AN ANFIELD
ANTHOLOGY

2000-2008

PAUL TOMKINS

For Matt and Adie.
For all the years spent on various motorways following
the Reds, and for doing most of the driving.
Cheers, guys.

And for William, Henry, Isabel, Luke and Stefan
— the next generation of Reds.

ISBN: 978-0-9556367-2-1

An Anfield Anthology
Published By Anchor Print Group

© Paul Tomkins
All rights reserved.
The moral right of the author has been asserted.

Printed in Great Britain by the Anchor Print Group Ltd.

First edition published 2008

CONTENTS

Pitchside

Introduction: Stuck In Pundit Hell

For me, and a number of other Liverpool fans, it's important how the Reds are treated within the media. I don't expect the club to receive constant glowing praise and to never be criticised, but I do want to see some balance. Just a little credit where it's due, as opposed to undeserved criticism and petty snipes.

The *Daily Telegraph* match report following the victory against Fulham in November 2007 was a case in point. It was basically written from the point of view that Liverpool, had they not scored two late goals to beat Fulham, would have drawn another game. (*Wow, really?*) And the piece suggested that drawing another game was not good enough, and certainly not championship form. Of course, let's not forget the awkward *fact* that it wasn't a draw, and that matches last at least 90 minutes. The last ten minutes are where the best teams often make it count. Anyone who has watched football for more than a month knows that.

Somehow it's okay for Manchester United to unconvincingly beat Spurs, Sunderland and Everton 1-0 with late or very late goals — that's "the sign of a great team". But Liverpool deservedly (as the only team intent on attacking) winning 2-0 with late goals is somehow just not good enough and the equivalent of a draw. Manchester United can draw two seasons running at non-league opposition in the FA Cup, but when Liverpool draw at League One Luton, it's another sign that Rafa Benítez just cannot do his job.

To put things into context, Alex Ferguson believes that his current crop is the best squad he's ever had. Yet the Reds are widely portrayed in the media as some second-rate outfit with no chance of the title in a million years — just as was said about their chances of getting anywhere in the Champions League in 2005 and 2007.

Something is wrong with this picture. If United are ever-improving (and to my mind they are), Chelsea have the most expensive squad in the history of the English game, and Arsenal are playing "the best football ever seen" (slightly facetious, but you know what I mean), then how come the Reds aren't getting at least some credit for still being within touching distance, while experiencing far more medium- and long-term injury problems? (All of a sudden Chelsea have a few players injured, and "injury crisis" has started appearing in the press.)

This Liverpool side, while not the finished article (and still prone to the odd lapse into mediocrity), is improving. The top four in England has been close to being the top four in *Europe* since Benítez arrived in England, (and includes the richest club in the world, if not the two richest, if United are included as well as Chelsea). Five years ago that was nowhere near the case. Even when Liverpool hammer someone, as they did with an 8-0 win against Besiktas, it's down to poor opposition; no-one said the same when Arsenal thrashed Slavia Prague 7-1. In each of his three full seasons Benítez has qualified for the Champions League, and recently made it past the group stage for the fourth time, and, with great distinction, to two finals.

While I'll never lose sleep over what's said in the papers or on the telly, views expressed in the media do still irritate me; they can become the mantra of many fans — particularly those who don't pay close attention to the facts but are quick to pick up their mobile and dial a phone-in — and add to the pressure on a manager and the team. Whatever happened to constructive criticism?

One of the drawbacks of not being able to get to many games these days, after a decade of being a season ticket holder, is that it leaves me, and my sanity, in the hands of the commentators. I frequently switch off the sound during live games, only to quickly need it back on to either hear the crowd (as it's unreal without it) or for an explanation of what's happening when the pictures aren't clear (such as when the director focuses on a vaguely attractive woman in the crowd; wow, a *woman*! — at a football match! — and she doesn't look like a man! Unbelievable!)

Craig Burley's comments about Benayoun during the Fulham game summed up the kind of football punditry that bugs me. Burley kept telling us that Benayoun needed to stay wide, to give the Reds some width. This is his opinion, and fair enough; although it could be argued that with the overlapping Arbeloa, the width was supplied by the full-back, as plenty of modern teams look to do. But then, when Benayoun picked up the ball in the middle of the field and drifted past a defender, Burley said "That's where Benayoun's at his best".

Er, *what?* — precisely where you've just spent 15 minutes telling us he shouldn't be? By all means have your opinion, but please stick to it for more than a quarter of a game.

I do think ex-players are good, and sometimes great, at analysing specific match situations with the video. But when it comes to the bigger picture, or to accepting new methods, they seem sadly lacking. They think like *players*, not managers — but it is managers who have to assess the overall tactical success. Players only really need concentrate on their own needs. They play for the team, but their primary instinct is self-interest. They're human. In his biography-cum-football philosophy book, *The Italian Job*, Gianluca Vialli made a big point about how he had to thoroughly change the way he thought about the game once he became a manager. But still the media employs mostly ex-players who haven't got the foresight to remove themselves from their insular playing mindsets, in order to think of the thousands of decisions that a manager has to weigh up going into every match.

For instance, when Alan Shearer assesses Benítez's tactics — such as playing Gerrard on the right — he focuses on how Gerrard feels. He is the kind of pundit who doesn't think about the juggling act a manager has to perform to get the best players on the pitch and to balance a team out. With all due respect to Shearer, who was a great centre-forward, what can he teach Rafa Benítez about tactics? I'm happy to hear what he has to say about what a striker should do in a certain position, but aside from helping out Glenn Roeder at Newcastle for a short while, when has he ever picked a team and it mattered? When has he signed a player? And no-one seemed to point out that Gerrard was actually playing well, scoring goals, and that — and this is the bottom line — Liverpool were winning games; something they weren't doing until Benítez switched the captain to the role. Gerrard wasn't being 'wasted'; he was doing a necessary job. And while Gerrard's mood is not irrelevant, the team was winning games; it didn't matter if the captain wasn't playing in his best position. He was playing in a position that was best for the team. In that situation it's down to the player to put his ego aside, and do what's best for the club he represents.

Meanwhile, Fernando Torres "should play every game", because Shearer wanted (and got) to play every game; despite not winning a single trophy in the final ten years of his career. Shearer admitted shouting at the TV monitor when Benítez took Torres off late in the game when on a hat-trick against

Portsmouth in December 2007; with the game won 4-1, Benítez was thinking about saving Torres for the next game, and winning that. Shearer was thinking only of personal glory: something that sums up his career.

There are a lot of pundits I respected during their time as players, and some of whom I would no doubt enjoy discussing football with. But too many, on top of not thinking like managers, do not see enough of Liverpool, and work on the easiest instincts — following the herd and rehashing received wisdom. Can we expect John Salako or Matt Le Tissier, covering a Liverpool game on Sky via a TV monitor, to have a great insight into the workings of the team and its manager when such ex-players might only occasionally cover the club? Is it not inevitable that such pundits — not necessarily known as great tactical thinkers or men with impressive IQs (or even common sense), while also possessing zero experience in management — will fall back on information they've heard through the grapevine, and trot out clichés? It's something I fell for during Claudio Ranieri's time as Chelsea manager: every pundit said he tinkered too much, therefore I concluded the same. Without actually watching Chelsea more than occasionally, how could I be qualified to justify such a viewpoint? I couldn't. But I learned a lesson as a result.

Information gets passed around this way, and it's hard to not automatically digest it. It really started to hit home for me when the debate on zonal marking from set-pieces started in 2004. At first I hated the system; the Reds were conceding goals, and looked a mess. And all the pundits — Andy Gray in particular — slated it. I got into a debate with an American Liverpool fan and football writer, who explained in more detail how the system works. Having only experienced man-marking while a player, I had no experience of zonal marking. And the only information I was getting via pundits was biased and negative. Towards the end of 2004, the Reds started to concede fewer and fewer goals from set-pieces. Then one or two would occur out of the blue, and suddenly zonal marking was lambasted again; all the while it had been working, no praise was offered. And it was only in 2006, when I started looking at the stats of the amount of set-piece goals conceded by the big clubs, that I saw that not only was it working for Liverpool, it led to the team conceding the fewest goals from free-kicks and corners delivered into the box. But even now, at the start of 2008, there is no praise for the system in the media, and only criticism.

With this in mind, I have grown increasingly less trustful of the experts put before us by Sky and their rivals. How many of these pundits are keen students of the game? I get the impression that it's not many. The problem is, those who are keen students of the game *stay in the game*; many of the talking head roles go to opinionated personalities — "characters" — who don't engage their brain before opening their mouth, plus a smattering of failed managers. At least Paul Merson had a go at being a manager; of course, he wasn't very good. (Why am I not surprised?)

While he's far from the best communicator, David Pleat at least offers an overview of the game from the perspective that matters most — that of the manager. Pleat's problem is that he doesn't have the kind of voice you can stand listening to for long. He can't get players' names right — who is this Benny Noon who plays on the right for Liverpool? — and he has little personality. But he understands football. His analyses sum up the difference between ex-players and ex-managers as pundits: the former tend to see only the smaller picture, and focus on individuals; the latter understand that the team is what matters most.

On the radio, Jimmy Armfield, while perhaps not in touch with the latest developments and practices and a little 'old school', offers a sturdier, more balanced approach than ex-players like Stan Collymore. Armfield is a man who led Leeds to a European Cup Final, in 1975; Collymore is a man famed for his mistakes in life, and for not being the sharpest tool in the box (even when he's the *only* tool in the box). Armfield has some idea, having been on both sides of the fence. Then there's someone like Alan Green, whom Armfield often works with, and who is all bluster and opinion, but seemingly little or no knowledge. Don't get me wrong — Green is a fantastic broadcaster; fellow BBC man, John Inverdale, said "You listen to Alan Green because you know that even if the game is as dull as ditchwater, the commentary won't be." He makes for great listening, providing it's not your team he's commenting on. If it is your team, then he shows his ignorance — because you then see the colourful commentaries for what they really are. And that's the problem. So while he's entertaining, he doesn't offer any insight — which, like Richard Keys, wouldn't be a problem if he stuck to an impartial or devil's advocate role, but as with Keys, he can't resist throwing in his own opinions. Speaking live about football, as commentators and summarisers have to do, is not easy: the foot and the mouth are unnaturally closely related when describing play. But there needs to be a consistency to what people are saying, and, as with phone-ins, more acknowledgement that they are pandering to the lowest common denominator, and chasing ratings — not truth, honesty and integrity. The saying "don't let the truth get in the way of a good story" is all too obvious.

Green and Keys are like the football writer who may love the game, but who has no idea about the sport he covers. He (or she) may be intelligent, and a talented writer, not to mention a good journalist (in terms of digging up stories and getting scoops), but that doesn't mean he'll have any intrinsic footballing know-how running through his veins or has ever kicked a football in his life. It doesn't mean he can accurately assess the game. In between there are a fair few insightful pundits and writers, but a lot of Liverpool fans do seem disillusioned with the way the club is represented.

But that doesn't mean ex-managers are any better at times. Following the 8-o win against Besiktas, in which Yossi Benayoun scored a hat-trick, Graeme Souness, speaking on TV, said that the Israeli was not good enough to play for Liverpool. Which, of course, might be more of a valid criticism had Souness, during his three years in charge, signed more than just *one* player who was definitely good enough: Rob Jones. (If you're being very generous you might throw in Mark Wright, too, who looked the part on his better days — notably after Souness left.) Maybe it's just me, but it irks that a man who got it as wrong in the transfer market as did Souness — and at a time when he was able to break the British transfer record, as he did with Dean Saunders (something Benítez hasn't been able to get close to), and also spent fees that were almost as large on a number of other players — can be critical of the current manager *buying a player for a relatively modest fee who is clearly better than most of his own judgement calls between 1991 and 1994.*

You would think that someone who constructed his own glass house would not have the temerity to throw rice, let alone stones. Souness understands how difficult the job is; but unlike Benítez, he made a complete and total pig's ear of the task, from start to end. That is not to say that Souness didn't inherit a difficult situation, with Dalglish bequeathing an ageing side, but to offload some of its better players and replace them with the likes of Stewart, Saunders, Kozma, Piechnik, Clough, Ruddock, Dicks, Walters, *et al*, surely leaves your opinion as *impotent* rather than important? Souness the player was imperious; Souness the manager was disastrous. It's not my job to say who has the right to express his or her views, as people will no doubt question my right in reply. But seriously, wouldn't you expect someone with as woeful a record in the transfer market as Souness to scuttle into a dark corner and hide, or at least bite his tongue, rather than publicly criticising one of his successors — who just happens to have done infinitely better in the league and Europe, having won the European Cup and reached another final?

You don't hear Kenny Dalglish being critical — like Souness, he understands how difficult the job is. But unlike Souness, he proved rather good at it. And he has shown infinitely more class in respecting the current incumbent.

These days, rather than write straight match reports, I concentrate on the bigger picture, and what surrounds each game: the form overall of the team and players; the tactics and systems; the short- or long-term patterns that can be picked out with statistics, or from watching games over and over on the video; and so on. While passionate about the club, I work hard to remove the excess passion that can cloud the issue and distort common sense.

And I guess I also look to provide what could be called a 'mediawatch' service, where I look to redress the balance from some of the more outlandish things said about the team.

For instance, on Sky's *The Sunday Supplement*, Paul Hayward of the *Daily Mail* accused Benítez of rotating because of his ego — "it's all about him and his rotation"; rotation that is undertaken, he said, to prove how clever he is.

Presumably Benítez's two titles and Uefa Cup with Valencia, and his European and FA Cups with Liverpool — won while using these methods — were merely to prove how clever he is? (Well, actually, it does suggest he might be *fairly* clever when it comes to this management lark.)

Quite what gives a journalist, whose cleverness is confined to the keyboard and who has never picked a team in his life, the right to make such an accusation is baffling. I've never known of a manager who'd rather prove his cleverness in any way other than winning games and, subsequently, trophies. Managers are obsessive winners. They'd feign a heart attack if their granny was going to beat them at tiddlywinks.

In three years, Benítez has reached four finals and achieved the Reds' highest points tally since 1988, *with rotation*. With just five unchanged teams in his 200 games, Rafa's win-rate of 56% bears comparison with the club's greats. It is fractionally behind Bob Paisley's, at 57%, but quite a way ahead of Bill Shankly's, at 51%. Only Kenny Dalglish's, at 60%, is significantly higher since John McKenna's 61% way back in the 1890s.

As for Benítez's ego, we're not talking about another Jose Mourinho, for whom the limelight was the only place to be, but a far lower-key man, who preaches the power of the collective, not the culture of the individual. But because he has 'ideas' — ideas that he has the temerity to stick to in the face of press criticism — he's an egotist? It's laughable.

"The fans are fed up with his rotation" said Hayward. Well, some fans may well be. But that doesn't mean we all are; or that those who are fed up are right and the rest of us wrong. The trouble is if you listen to phone-ins for the opinion of 'real fans', you are likely to get the most controversial opinions, as that's what the producers want. The views of the fans of any one club vary quite wildly; as such I've never tried to represent "the fans" as a whole, just present my own views.

Another theory espoused by Hayward — which the *Daily Mirror*'s Oliver Holt did well to debunk — was that the European Cup now means nothing to Liverpool fans, who want the Premiership title.

Holt was spot-on when he argued that the European Cup has a special place in Liverpool's history and in the hearts of its fans. It's almost being treated as if it counts for nothing now, in order to find a reason to slate Benítez as a failure. I'm sorry, but the European Cup meant plenty to Liverpool fans while the Reds were winning it, and arguably even more between 1985 and 2005, when repeating the feat had become the most spindly of pipe dreams as we looked on in envy. Yes, the Premier League is desired after such a long wait, and to some has become an obsession, but the Champions League cannot be devalued as a result. If success in the league is not forthcoming, success in Europe is no small consolation.

It may sound paranoid, but if Manchester United had been doing as well in Europe while they weren't winning the league (such as between 2003 and 2007) there would be no such criticisms of the competition meaning so little. I mean, Ferguson has only made one final in the 15 years United have been consistently qualifying for it, and despite being *desperate* for a second success. This from a man whose first five seasons in the English league ended with United finishing 11th, 2nd, 11th, 13th, and 6th!

And while the league title has yet to return to Anfield, before Rafa arrived the Reds' league form meant the club weren't even qualifying for the Champions League every season — something he has a 100% record with.

I do think as fans we can be oversensitive to some of criticisms of the club we hold dear, as it can be like hearing someone bad-mouth your wife or your mother — but while some of it will be fair (no manager, player or club gets everything right), so much of it can be ludicrous.

I had to laugh at Paul Hayward yet again (for his second successive appearance) launching a surreal attack on Benítez on Sky's *Sunday Supplement* at the end of 2007. This time it was "Benítez doesn't deserve any money in the transfer window" — a quite bizarre statement. Who is he to say which manager deserves to spend his own club's money? The conclusion was that Rafa would "only go and spend it on a couple of Spanish players anyway".

Which is interesting — perhaps even xenophobic. Of Benítez's previous 16 senior signings at the time, only four were from Spain, and only two Spanish. Talk about stereotyping someone. Five of those 16 signings were from the Premiership, while others have been from France, Holland, Brazil, Argentina, Denmark and Germany. I can't imagine someone would say of Arsene Wenger, in a sneering tone, that he'd just go and buy a couple of French players if you gave him some money. Benítez did spend £6.5m in the transfer window, on Martin Skrtel — a Slovakian playing for Zenit St. Petersburg, in Russia.

People did criticise Gérard Houllier for buying too many players from France, and as a result, Benítez was instantly tarred with the same brush when starting out with Spanish signings in 2004. But the difference was that not one of Houllier's French signings was an outright success. A couple did fairly well, but that was as good as it got; most were flops. Houllier failed to do what his compatriot, friend and rival at Highbury was doing. Whereas Wenger tapped the French market initially, because it was a) what he knew best and b) where there were some great talents, Benítez understandably did the same with Spain. Not only did he know those players, but they also knew and respected him. Why did Torres join Liverpool in 2007, when he had the chance to join other English teams beforehand? Clearly, as well as Liverpool's prestige, it was the Spanish connection.

Wenger signed some horrible duds and mediocre talents from France, but we only remember those few top-class ones who succeeded. That's how the best managers operate: they make mistakes, but they get it right often enough. No-one needed to recall Kaba Diawara once Thierry Henry arrived; no-one mentioned Christopher Wreh because there was Robert Pires; and Pascal Cygan can be forgotten on account of the success of Gael Clichy.

Benítez has gone to Spain to recruit Alonso, Garcia, Reina, Arbeloa and Torres: five top-class players for well below £50m. And the last name in that list could well be the Footballer of the Year, at his current rate of progress. He also bought Josemi, Gonzalez, Kromkamp Pellegrino and Morientes from his home league, but for just a little over £10m combined, and recouped most of that when offloading them soon after.

There seems to be a culture of 'I know best' surrounding football; as was the case with Noel White, the Liverpool Director who resigned after tactical criticisms in the winter of 2006. Everyone is entitled to his or her own opinion, *but that does not make it valid or correct*; take a tribesman from a remote part of the Amazon rain forest to see his first ever match, and he may have an opinion, but it won't mean he understands the game. It's the same with fans — some who go to the game every week know a lot, others don't. You could give a monkey a season ticket, but he wouldn't be able to give you a valued critique.

Managers have to be trusted and left to get on with their jobs. They are the experts. Otherwise it's like taking your car to a mechanic and telling him how to fix it, even though you've never once got your hands dirty under the bonnet. Theory is all well and good, but in football only the manager's theories can ever be tested. You should only cry foul if, as in the classic Seinfeld episode, the mechanic steals the car and takes it on a reckless joyride across the country. I try to examine why a Liverpool manager does something, but not from the point of view of knowing better or having all the answers. And if that makes me a dull writer, I'd rather be dull and stick to my principles and try to retain some integrity than pander to typical media hysteria where everything is always black or white. Sometimes it's just another shade of grey, and that's fine by me.

While I think I've become more patient and understanding as a 'football analyst', and can see how managing Liverpool to a level that would please everyone is an almost impossible task, I think my judgement has proven fairly accurate over the years. This book contains writing from Gérard Houllier's time in charge, but my disillusionment with the manager, between 2002 and 2004, was kept to a private forum, partly out of a desire to not spend my time carping about what I felt were increasingly one-dimensional tactics, and partly because events in my personal life meant I had neither the energy or the inclination to write proper articles at the time.

I now wonder how much of my own frustration, anxiety, depression and anger came through in those forum assessments; probably a fair amount. But anyone who knew me from that can attest that, as far as history panned out, I lost faith at just about the right time. In contrast to my current label, I was even accused of being a pessimist. It takes more than a few games to decide that a manager has lost the plot, or taken a team as far as it can go, and it seems that knee-jerk reactions can beset even the best managers, as Rafael Benítez has continually discovered. A bad season can befall any manager; two in a row is more worrying.

Even now, I don't pretend to know better than Gérard Houllier, and I still think the first few years of his reign were largely excellent. But he had lost the majority of the fans, and also, perhaps even more crucially, the players themselves: Michael Owen and Steven Gerrard were not happy with the way things were going, and Benítez's first job was to try and keep the best two players of his inheritance. Also, Houllier was a manager who let the coaches take the training; Benítez is a manager-coach, who has much more of a positive influence on the team as a result. Houllier had six years in charge, and by the summer of 2004 there was a definite air of stagnation. Teams like Southampton and Charlton were winning league games at Anfield, and the European form had dramatically worsened year-on-year from 2001, to the point where the Reds were doing poorly in the Uefa Cup, and then missing out on Europe entirely.

The key is to not start thinking this is the case for every manager after a few bad results; there's a big difference between a dip and careering into a chasm from which there's no escape. After six years in charge, and with a budget similar to his rivals (until 2003 at least, when Roman Abramovich pitched up), Houllier had been given ample opportunity. Benítez, meanwhile, has to face a super-rich Chelsea as well as strong Manchester United and Arsenal sides.

I have continued to defend Benítez's approach, through some difficult patches, because at this point in time I still think he is the best man for the job. Am I a hypocrite? I hope not. I see Benítez as very different from Houllier. First of all, Houllier wasn't anywhere near as 'proven' as Benítez: he had one prior league title win, in 1986, some 12 years before he arrived at Anfield; compared with Benítez's two in three years, very much against the odds. The Spaniard added something more remarkable to his CV, with his Champions League success in 2005. (Houllier did subsequently win two league titles with Lyon, but he had inherited the *only* top-class team in France. It was a fine achievement, but not a remarkable one.)

Then there was Houllier's illness in 2001: a distinct point where you could at least attribute blame for the change. Maybe it had absolutely no affect on him whatsoever, and his limits had already been reached. But the dissected aorta offered a clear before-and-after scenario. While Houllier seemed to have only one approach, Benítez has shown far greater tactical flexibility. The accusations levelled at the Spaniard have been regarding *too much* flexibility: different tactics and rotated personnel. And maybe he does overcook things at times, but then that has also brought a lot of success. So while I don't think any manager is above criticism, I do think that you have to look into all the reasons behind any supposed failure, as well as keeping that criticism fair and realistic, and free from "I know better".

One thing I've learned lately is that it's very difficult to say for sure where a team is in terms of its transition, and how near it is to completion. The examples of Arsenal and Manchester United between 2003 and 2006/7 have taught me a lot about how to view these things. Having been at the forefront of the league for a number of years, both teams seemed to have lost their way. But look at them now.

United's renaissance took place at the start of last season, taking many people by surprise, while Arsenal have done the same this season. The development came when most of the elements were finally in place after many years of work: the team increasingly gelled and individuals matured.

Both Ferguson and Wenger had began rebuilding in earnest in 2003 and 2004, but had of course been laying the groundwork since the '90s; gaining a leap on Benítez by signing some outstanding young players.

By 2006, it appeared that Benítez's Reds had overtaken Arsenal and drawn level with Manchester United. But while Liverpool had undoubtedly improved, the situation was deceptive; it was around this point that young players like Ronaldo, Rooney, Van Persie, Fabregas, Adebayor and Toure really started to come of age, developing into some of the best players in the country. And after two unremarkable seasons where he looked like £10m wasted, Hleb suddenly clicked into gear.

It may be an obvious metaphor, but Wenger and Ferguson had planted some acorns prior to Benítez's arrival in England, and it took a while for them to become formidable oaks. They were able to do this as part of an evolution, whereas Benítez initially had to look for more instant solutions, to make the Reds competitive, but often on a fairly tight budget that limited his scope.

In a sense, Benítez is approaching the stage now where it should all begin to click into place. After a first season of assessment, he has been able to add a collection of top-class and world-class young players. Some of them are still at the acorn or sapling stage, but others are fully formed.

I've read a lot of nonsense about Liverpool being light years behind the top sides, on account of the head-to-heads with those rivals. It makes no sense, particularly as two were drawn (one thanks to a woeful refereeing decision) and one lost pretty much against the run of play.

While these were all home games, Liverpool are now far better equipped to go on the road and do to these teams what they did at Anfield: namely get men behind the ball and hit on the counter attack with great pace. That is the greatest development at Liverpool this season. By contrast, the home form — so good for three seasons — has been unusually poor, and while that's a concern, I honestly can't see that remaining the case for long.

After the Manchester United game there was talk of the Reds being "two top-class players short". Of course, without the injured Agger and Alonso (who's now back, but still feeling his way to peak fitness), amongst other absentees, that was true in a way that such statements didn't intend. And it was a game where the narrowest of margins separated the sides. United got the confidence boost; Liverpool the kick in the teeth.

While there may be the odd exception to the rule, it takes a team with a number of new elements time to gel. If Torres was good earlier in the season, he's looking sensational now; and at 23 he will almost certainly get better, as an individual and, once his team-mates know him better, as a threat to the opposition.

He took to the league quickly, but has become more of a match-winner as the season has progressed. At a stage of the year when a lot of new players start to wilt, he has got stronger; *perhaps* because Rafa didn't overplay him earlier in the campaign. He's looked tired at times, as most players do over Christmas, but the goals are flowing.

It is true that you can build an outstanding team on a tighter budget. But it takes longer. First you have to scout the right youngsters, sign them, and wait for them to mature. Or you have to wait for the right older players to become available at a good price: either because they're out of contract, or in the case of a player like Arbeloa, because no-one else has quite realised how good he is. This is what irritates me about statements like "Wenger's built a great team for peanuts"; first of all, this Arsenal team has not won anything of note as yet (though it might), and second, Wenger has had time to cultivate his crop.

You only need look at the improvements made by Everton in the last year or two in relation to how it takes time. David Moyes has spent a reasonable amount of money, but is now firmly established at Goodison Park after taking control in 2002. He endured some horrible seasons as the club yo-yoed dramatically in his first four years, but now there's some consistency and stability. Even so, it's a club that has not had to build to sustain the rigours of a league campaign combined with Champions League; it's that much harder when you get to that level, and have to maintain competitiveness in the Premiership and against the best teams in Europe.

An interesting example of this 'I know best' phenomenon could be seen in a 2006 episode of Gordon Ramsey's *Kitchen Nightmares*. The intimidating Ramsey, once on the books of Glasgow Rangers, is clearly not a man to be messed with. He is also one of the world's most successful chefs — a bit like a culinary version of Bob Paisley in that he has achieved the nigh-impossible three Michelin Stars. Not only has he run his own successful restaurants, he has turned around many ailing ones on the programme in question. On a visit to Spain, to help rescue an eatery that was going down the pan, he ended butting up against a 26-year-old who, despite very little experience and a business hemorrhaging money at an alarming rate, seemed to be of the opinion that he himself knew best. (You see the same thing on property development shows, too. Get the expert in, then ignore them.) Ramsey's way of proving his point was to put the young man in a bullring; extreme, perhaps, but sometimes it takes severe measures to get through. Faced with an angry young bull and armed with just his scarlet cloak, the petrified young restaurateur did have an expert close by, to feed him advice. Funnily enough, he took it.

By the same token, some loud-mouthed fans and pundits — those who don't so much as offer an opinion but think they know best — should be dropped into the deep end and put in charge of a massive club for a week, month or even a season. Of course, no big club would contemplate such a suicidal stunt. But how would such people cope with the realities of running a team? — such as attacks from all angles of the media and the stands; dealing with 20-40 professionals, all of whom want to be in the starting XI, and some of whose agents are continually destabilising them; trying to buy the players you want, and the myriad ways you can be foiled; having to explain your ideas to the board, when the board will inevitably have less, little or no football knowledge; planning tactics, substitutions, and dealing with injuries, particularly to key people; watching reliable players making human errors that cost the game; having to be a father, brother, friend, confidant and psychologist to a big group of men with large egos; and so on.

My understanding of what a football manager has to face has grown; and how, when things are going wrong, there's no magic wand to wave. It's easy to suggest changes, but the manager cannot control every aspect of any given game — the opposition's inspired form on the day; the referee's unbelievable blindness; the inexplicable mistakes good players make; and the luck that all sportsmen need. Once things start to go wrong in a game the adverse circumstances can quickly take on a life-force of their own. No wonder most managers end up looking insane on the touchline.

Istanbul proved that even the direst situations can be turned around, but such occurrences are rare. And it showed that luck, and getting your team's fortunes to take on a life-force of their own, plays a big part. In 2007, Liverpool outplayed AC Milan but lost; in 2005, Liverpool were comprehensively outplayed for all but 15 minutes in 2005, and won.

It wasn't one single thing that led Liverpool to that glorious victory, contrary to the way it is often accredited to the introduction of Didi Hamann at half-time. It also required a quick goal to instil belief and to suggest it might not be a mere consolation; it required the AC Milan players to switch off after half-time, and to momentarily crumble once they conceded; it required individuals in red to step up to the mark, in the way Steven Gerrard, Jamie Carragher and Jerzy Dudek clearly did; and it required the narrow margins between success and failure to fall the Reds' way: if Milan Baros hadn't managed to get out of the way of Vladimir Smicer's shot by a matter of inches, the revival could have all come to nothing. The same with Andrei Shevchenko's late miss: it required an outstanding reflex save from Dudek, but an inch or two either way, and the keeper would have been powerless to intercede. And what about John Arne Riise's cross that led to the first goal: had the first cross not been blocked it could have sailed harmlessly into Dida's arms. In getting that first cross wrong — in other words, in making a mistake — it fortunately rolled back invitingly to the Norwegian to try again. This time it coincided perfectly with Gerrard's run.

While Gerrard getting into the box would have been part of the second-half tactics, Benítez had very little control, if any, on that series of events. Even though it is not his style, he could have passionately orated the most Churchillian of speeches at the interval — fight them on the beaches, fight them on the halfway line, etc, as well as throwing teacups and head-butting the wall — and a quick, lucky goal against the run of play from the Italians would have rendered it irrelevant. However, no speech at all, and a quick, lucky goal in the Reds' favour could have inspired the players more than even the most astutely chosen words. As I said earlier, a game of football often takes on a life-force of its own.

As watching fans, we think we could effect changes by making substitutions or tactical alterations, but there's nothing to say they would make the slightest difference, or that things wouldn't actually get worse, even if they seemed fairly logical calls. A manager doesn't have full control of his own players. He cannot move the players into the exact positions he requires for the entire 90 minutes, nor can he think for them, or magically provide them with confidence if it's lacking. Too many quick fixes are offered by fans and those pundits who don't spend long enough thinking about what they are saying: change X and Y, and Bob's your uncle. Job done, problem solved. If only it were that easy. Of course, if it was, more of these people would become managers, and would all be incredibly successful (ignoring, of course, that there is a limit to how many clubs can be successful in any given season.) The more I write about the game, the more I discover what I don't yet know. Some people may label football a simple game, but that's only the case if you're a genius like Bob Paisley, and you've already accumulated a wealth of knowledge along the way. Rather than always saying what's right, I try to argue with those who say something is *definitely* wrong — this or that certainly doesn't work, and will never work, and so on. I don't claim to know best, as clearly I don't. But I do know when certain statements made in the media are purposefully incendiary, and when opinions are given as 'absolutes'.

Speaking on Liverpool FC TV in December 2007, the *Daily Mirror*'s Brian Reade, with some insider knowledge, said that he felt there was a mainstream media agenda against Rafa Benítez. He cited the fact that a lot of journalists at the time suggested Liverpool, as one of the country's major clubs, should have appointed an Englishman, such as Alan Curbishley or Sam Allardyce (I ask you...). Here was another foreigner coming in, and to make matters worse, it was one who wasn't happy to indulge the media in their favourite games, unlike the more charismatic Jose Mourinho.

Maybe Liverpool's problems would all have been solved if the Liverpool board had taken the advice of those pressmen in 2004, and appointed, say, Steve McClaren instead ...

Liverpool's Summer Transfer Activity Explained
July 2005

I've noticed a pattern: every summer the same discussions arise. Two opposing arguments will be proffered on every possible signing: He's *too* this, or He's *not enough* that.

"Yeah, but . . ."

"Shut it, dickhead. He's crap. *End of.*"

Ultimately, it's the individual player in question who matters. We all look to what has gone before (at times I'm as guilty as anyone), but there is never a perfect precedent. Just because Player X didn't adapt to the Premiership, it doesn't mean Player Y won't either. He might not, of course. But he is his own man, in a different period of time, and in a different set of circumstances. He is not a clone. You cannot replicate the situation as it was in the past, or even come close.

Signing a Scottish international from Celtic does not mean you get the next Kenny Dalglish. Signing an old baldy fella from Coventry does not get you another Gary McAllister. Still, it doesn't stop the repetition of stock arguments.

"He's Just A One Season Wonder"

Any player who has done well the previous season, but not beforehand, gets labelled the One Season Wonder. Almost always a striker, he will be compared with Marcus Stewart, Kevin Phillips (somewhat bizarrely, as he was rather better than that), Michael Ricketts (how did he looks so good for a while, and end up so spectacularly bad?) and Andy 'How Many Penalties?' Johnson. [*Who is now a two season wonder.*]

Of course, sometimes you cannot afford to wait for a player to be a 14-season wonder — making your move at the precise moment he announces his retirement.

Then there's the issue of improvement: as a player's game clicks into place, for one reason or another. Is Peter Crouch improving dramatically, or did he merely have a good six months? (In a crap side, at that.) Bad and lucky players do not score 16 goals in 24 Premiership games in a poor team. Even the best players in the world, in the form of their lives, wouldn't do much better than two goals every three league games.

Would Crouch do better with players like Gerrard, Alonso, Luis Garcia, Kewell, Gonzales, Zenden and Figo (hopefully) supplying the service? You can but assume it would surpass a pass from Rory Delap. And how can you judge a player who had to play for Graham Taylor at Aston Villa, with one who would play for Rafa Benítez at Liverpool? Same freakishly tall human being with comedy teeth, but one whose ability to succeed depends on working with a manager who can bring the best out of him. It is like giving lumps of clay to both Michelangelo and a monkey to see which one can manufacture something aesthetically pleasing. (Admittedly, Michelangelo has been dead for 441 years, and as such, the metaphor is slightly ill conceived; unless, of course, to even it out, the monkey has also been dead for 441 years — in which case, the whole thing is just rather macabre: a dead artist, a dead monkey and two untouched pieces of clay . . .)

The opposite argument is "He's Crap Now, He's Lost It"; to be used for any player who hasn't scored a goal for three weeks.

"He's Too Old/Past His Best"

A perennial, this old chestnut. The current debate surrounds Luis Figo. Class is permanent, after all — although even the best players head over the hill at some point, and descend rapidly down the other side. Figo remains a quality act, and is still fit, professional and dedicated. It's a bit like moaning that your old Ferrari "only does 220mph these days . . .". Ultimately it remains better than even the top-range Skoda.

Then again, if the Ferrari won't even start, as the engine spontaneously combusted (although isn't that what the internal combustion engine is supposed to do?), then even the most basic, fully-functioning Skoda would be a better choice to get from A to B.

Of course, there's always Mauricio Pellegrino. He didn't do so good, did he? Big reputation, but on the slide. Bit like Laurent Blanc at Manchester United.

Sure, but don't forget Gary McAllister.

Ah, but Pellegrino . . .

And repeat.

Good examples, and bad examples. I say potato, you say *pot-tah-toe*. I say McAllister, you say Pellegrino. Both are right. Neither are right. Bergkamp and Zola remain prime examples of players still cutting it in their mid-to-late 30s. There are other players who looked past it at 29. One last payday, or a legend with a point to prove? It's all about the individual.

"He's Too Expensive"

People like to assign players a set value, from which they are not allowed to deviate. Peter Crouch is apparently worth only £2.91758m in the eyes of most Liverpool fans, but worth over twice that to the Liverpool manager. Why?

The way I see it, Rafa has a set budget, which we are not aware of, and a hit-list of players on whom to spend that money. If he gets all the players he wants within the overall budget: bingo. That's all he cares about. Is Peter Crouch worth £7m? If he is to Rafa, then he is to me. (Unless I'm being asked to foot the full bill; in which case he's a lanky streak of piss, and I can spare a fiver at most.)

Seriously though, if Rafa can spend a total of £7m on Figo, Zenden and Crouch, at an average of less than £3m each, then it doesn't matter which one cost £7m and which two were free? Three internationals, two of whom have achieved many, many things in the game, and another who appears to be coming good at a relatively young age. Of course, the higher the price tag, the more pressure on the individual to justify it. But again, that's down to the individual, and you don't know if a player can handle that until he has the chance to. If he failed after previous big(ish) money moves, then that could be for myriad reasons.

Also see: "He's Too Cheap". As in "He only cost £3m or less, he can't be any good." (Josemi, Nunez . . . Um, Hyypia, Henchoz, Riise, Baros, McAllister, Babbel.) [Interestingly, this was Alan Hansen's argument in October 2006.]

"Only A Reserve At Another Club"

One man's meat is another man's poison. Or in other words, what works for some may not work for others. Is Michael Owen any worse now than 12 months ago, despite being third choice at Real Madrid? Can you compare the standard of player between a reserve at Barcelona and a first team player at Birmingham?

This particular argument surfaced twice in the summer of 2004: it was used to denigrate Antonio Nunez, and yet Luis Garcia — who would become Liverpool's star in the knock-out phases of the Champions League, and joint top-scorer overall — was only a squad player at Barcelona, even before Deco and Guily arrived. Luis Garcia may be a far better player than Nunez; but neither were in their respective teams' first XI. Again, it depends on the individual, not their situation. Fernando Morientes was another who lost his first-team place at Real Madrid, but remains a class act.

The same can be said of one outgoing transfer: Alou Diarra. Good enough to play for France (although not a first choice, of course), but at Liverpool he was behind Gerrard, Alonso and Hamann. No wonder he opted to play first team football in France with the World Cup looming. Had Gerrard and Hamann left Liverpool this summer, along with Biscan, Diarra might have become a key player. Some teams are especially strong in one area, and at Liverpool that has been the case with central midfielders. You can't ask ambitious players to hang around as fourth or fifth choices for long.

A reserve at a big club can be a great player in need of an opportunity.

"Never Played For A Big Club"

Actually, this is one of my own favourites. While not essential, it's always helpful if a player has experienced the unique pressures of life at a big club: the bigger, more demanding crowds who expect success; the existence of a whole host of legends from the past to live up to; the regular appearances in European football; the extra press attention; and, of course, the likelihood of squad rotation, which brings its own challenge to confidence.

But even great players often have to make the step up at some stage. Juventus signed Zidane from Bordeaux, and the bonus was that he was a bargain. Real Madrid then bought Zidane after his first experience of a big club, and it cost them £46m. Juventus got the Frenchman's best years, and outstanding value for money.

"We Must Sign World-Class Players"

Always a good one, and certain to lead to a three-day debate as to what defines 'world-class'. World-class players, if (loosely) defined as the very best 50 players in the world (and not just those who grace the world stage now and then), tend to cost £20m upwards. Not to mention £20m+ in wages over a four-year contract.

Someone — usually aged 15 — will get overexcited and go too far as, high from the fumes of unchanged underpants, he suggests the manager should sign Robinho, Robben, Ronaldo, Ronaldinho and Ronald McDonald. The words 'Championship Manager' will appear in reply soon after.

All teams need the best players it can get its hands on: providing they fit into the scheme of things. Real Madrid remain the perfect example of how buying the best players without any great masterplan can result in declining standards. World-class players demand world-class wages. If their egos are oversized, and they drag their weight rather than pull it, they can destabilise a club.

"No Premiership Experience/Might Not Settle"

Always a good one to pull from the bag to write off any potential signing who happens to be from another country. Every signing is a gamble: the same is as true of those from England as those from overseas. Clearly overseas players will need the possible period of adaptation, but it's not like anyone's asking them to switch from football to blindfolded tobogganing.

Apparently suited to the English game: Salif Diao. Patently unsuited to the English game: Luis Garcia. While they are clearly different types of player, sometimes *good* players are all you need; the rest will take care of itself in due course. Better to get someone like Robert Pires working with the dedication of a Salif Diao, as you'll never get a Diao playing with the skill of a Pires.

"He Wouldn't Get Into the Chelsea or Arsenal Side"

Always a bit misleading, this one. After all, Frank Lampard was Footballer of the Year, and yet many Reds would opt for Steven Gerrard and Xabi Alonso every time. Chelsea fans might argue that, given their parsimonious defence, which broke Liverpool's 1979 record for fewest goals conceded (in less games, mind), Jamie Carragher wouldn't get into their team. Chelsea are perfectly happy with Lampard, and Liverpool are delighted with Carragher. Neither club needs to buy their rival's best player from 2004/05: although you'd always try to find a place for them, somewhere, if given the option.

Ultimately this is about what Liverpool need; not what Chelsea or Arsenal do not need.

Conclusion

So basically, the ideal signing would be a player aged around 24/25, with Premiership experience, who was born overseas in a sunny clime (they are always more skilful, aren't they?) but who grew up in the English game, and who has played in the latter stages of the Champions League at a club with a large home crowd and a tradition of success, as well as experiencing international football.

I fed all the information into my high-powered computer (ZX Spectrum 48k with wonky rubber keys) and waited for 16 hours (in between a quick game of Horace Goes Skiing) for the results to print out, dot-matrix format, on thermal paper that looks more like loo roll.

According to those criteria, the best signing the club has made in the last 20 years is . . .

. . . Harry Kewell.

The Rotation Rope Tightens
October 2007

Give a man enough rope, the saying goes, and he will hang himself.

Or in other words, give him the opportunity and he will become the victim of his own folly.

But it's not Rafa who's hanging himself with rotation — it's the short-sighted media doing it for him. Like a man wrongly identified as a paedophile by people who forgot to check their facts, an angry mob is gathering, its ire based on misinformation fired by a media frenzy.

In a very public trial that never ends, Rafa, with his rotation policy, stands eternally accused.

Over the past couple of years I've given plenty of reasons why I think the criticism of rotation is wrong. But I think I've finally found the exact reason I loathe that criticism so much. And it has a lot to do with the legal system.

In the case of anyone accused of a serious crime, the defence does not need to prove anything. It is the prosecution which has to prove guilt *beyond a reasonable doubt*. The defence simply needs to show that reasonable doubt exists.

And so a man (and his rotation policy) should be innocent unless *proven* guilty.

At least that would be the concept in a criminal trial; a trial by media is something entirely different. No witnesses need to be called and evidence is not required — just gut instincts, suspicions and suppositions. Innocent until proven guilty has no part in the media.

In civil law cases, decisions are made on the 'balance of probabilities' — or whether something is more probable than not. But even this is impossible to determine with rotation, as you cannot compare the different team selections against the same opposition in the same circumstances. Each game, whoever plays, is unique. Cause and effect determines so much of what happens.

I am not necessarily trying to say that rotation is the only way to go. Indeed, you cannot conclusively prove that it *does* work — did you win because the team was rotated? Perhaps. But as with the opposite outcome, you cannot compare alternate scenarios. All you can do is allow the manager to select his team as he sees fit, and accept that in recent years, the title has been won with the manager making on average more than three changes per game.

So it comes down to this question: should Liverpool have clearly been the best team, the favourites to win the league in the last two seasons, only for 'tinkering' to have undone the natural strength of the team? The answer is no. All you can say is that, in terms of squad ability, and perceived strongest XI, the Reds should have been in the top three or four, which proved the case.

While I accept that a certain amount of rotation is essential in the modern game, I'm actually pretty ambivalent about the extent of it beyond that. It has pros and cons (as does the alternative), so to a large degree I can take it or leave it.

But I can't stress enough how utterly out of control the anti-rotation rhetoric has become. It's frightening. Anytime anything — any single thing — goes wrong at Liverpool, it's the fault of rotation. It thwarts all proper debate.

Rafa's rotation is the root of all evil. I'm just waiting to hear that Rafa's rotation was riding a moped down the *Pont d'Alma* underpass in Paris in August 1997, or was stood with a rifle on a grassy knoll in Dealey Plaza, Texas, in 1963.

Only a few weeks ago Mark Lawrenson was laying all the blame of a bad result at the feet of rotation. On *Football Focus* in early October, after the home draw against Spurs, he said "I'm afraid it's the rotation system again".

Then, when Rafa keeps faith in the same two strikers who played at the weekend for the Besiktas game (and he only had three to choose from), Lawrenson says on Five Live: "Rafael Benitez got his selection policy completely wrong. You saw what Crouch did. Within a minute of coming on he made the goal for Gerrard."

Now, Lawrenson may be correct in either one of these assumptions. But he cannot be correct on both.

To me it is yet another example of punditry by hindsight — of always being right and a manager wrong, by suggesting, after the event, the opposite of what the manager actually did, preferably with a condescending tone of superiority. It's inconsistent, hypocritical punditry that involves paying no attention to what you've said before. Any muppet can do that.

If Benítez had started Crouch in Turkey, he'd have been rotating. Had Liverpool still lost, or Crouch had a poor game, Lawrenson and his ilk would no doubt have blamed the lack of continuity up front: "I'm afraid it's the rotation system again".

But with Torres out injured, Rafa went with the two strikers who share nine goals this season, not the striker who has just one (admittedly from limited chances). I mean, fancy doing something crazy like that?

A post by someone on the 606 Forum appeared on the main BBC football site: "I think Rafa needs to scrap his rotation policy once and for all ... or we need to scrap him. Anyone agree?" It's typical of the mood amongst many so-called fans. It's mob mentality, with the lowest possible IQ.

This came during a game in Turkey where Benítez had made just two changes following the derby, dropping Momo Sissoko, whom everyone said needed removing after a poor game, to bring in the more attack-minded Pennant, and replacing Benayoun with Babel, which, given both are flair players, is pretty much like-for-like. So, a more attacking team on balance, and one in which Babel, who was introduced to the side, did particularly well.

At first it was zonal marking that was Benítez's crazy continental folly, but most Liverpool fans have come to see that the team actually concede very few goals from set pieces delivered into the box. In fact, barely any.

But even now, to highlight the ignorance of pundits who only catch Liverpool games here and there, Andy Gray only ever says negative things like "there's the problem with zonal marking…".

He did this against Besiktas when a Turkish centre-back found himself with an incredibly difficult shooting chance towards the angle of the 18-yard box. "It could so easily have gone in the top corner," Gray said, as the ball sailed into space. Yeah, Andy, if it was Marco Van Basten shooting.

The only goal Pepe Reina has conceded from a corner or free-kick into the box this season was against Everton. The original corner was dealt with (to a degree), but the ball was put back in from the other side of the area. And even then, the problem wasn't an unmarked Evertonian because of zonal marking — it was Sami Hyypia thinking *he* was Marco Van Basten. Hyypia was perfectly placed to deal with the cross, but he scored an own goal when attempting to clear. Shit happens.

The rotation debate started with people saying "rotation is rubbish" when Liverpool lost games, even if the result came about from bad refereeing, poor finishing, human error, or a freakish own goal.

Once Rafa stood accused, the council for the defence, of which I am a willing volunteer, stepped forward to ask the prosecution for *proof* that rotation definitely doesn't work. But have they provided any? No.

While the media hasn't been able to get a bandwagon going over zonal marking for a year or two now, the more complex and 'unprovable' issue of rotation rumbles on.

And yet the more I delve into rotation — looking into the issue in infinitely more detail than I've seen anyone else in the media bother to — the more evidence I find that suggests it works; or, at the very least, that it's far from the folly so many would have us believe.

I'm never going to say it's perfect, but then no team selection can ever be said to be perfect before any game; you can only make judgements afterwards, and that's a luxury a manager doesn't have.

Oliver Anderson, a statistician with whom I have been working for a couple of years, is now producing stats on all Premiership teams, and trends within the entire division. For a compay called The Football Review, he has produced a book and a website that looks at a variety of statistics, most of which I think are very meaningful. In particular, his stuff on rotation is very revealing.

From my own research, I was aware that, in the league last season,

Liverpool won their most points, on average, when Rafa made three changes. And I'd also pointed out that Liverpool made the same amount of Premiership changes as Manchester United last season (118, at just over three per game), which was also the exact same amount made by Chelsea the year before.

And unlike all the media hacks, I had also previously pointed out that, when it comes to Alex Ferguson supposedly never rotating his main men while Rafa always tinkers with his key players, the fact was that Gerrard, Reina and Carragher all started more league games in 2006/07 than any Man United player.

But it's interesting to look at the trend across the entire Premiership. Changes may also be due to injury or suspension, but it all goes to show the need for the "same XI this week lads" that so many old-timers suggest is essential is an utter myth when it comes to the modern game.

Last season there were 380 Premiership matches, which means 760 team line-ups. Only 83 of them were unchanged from the previous league game; a massive 677 involved altered team-sheets.

Across the league as a whole, when managers kept an unchanged team they on average won 37% of matches. Managers who made none, one or two changes to their line-ups also won 37%.

But managers who made between three and seven changes won 41% — a fairly significant improvement. Indeed, mirroring the amount of unchanged line-ups, there were also 83 times when managers made four changes, and the win-rate then was over 42%. Compare that with the 83 times no changes were made, and tell me this stat is irrelevant?

There could be a million reasons why all these results occurred, ranging from luck to inspired judgement, but it clearly shows that changing a team does not automatically lead to failure. Last season, a team was actually far more likely to win with four changes than with none.

Perhaps Rafa has rotated too much this season. And on occasion maybe he got his line-up wrong, inasmuch as you can say we'd have done better had he made other selections (which, of course, you can't for certain).

But he's also had disruptive injuries to Gerrard, Carragher, Kewell (okay, he's always injured, but all the same he's a player Rafa wants to use), and more recently, Agger, Alonso and Torres. Now for me, they are six of the eight most talented footballers on the books. Gerrard and Carragher both lost their form with their injuries. Not because of rotation.

I'm sure Rafa would want to stick to a more settled core, or spine, to his side, as he did in recent seasons, but five of the six players I've just listed represent that spine. So how can he possibly find the core consistency he wants if players are out injured, or struggling after injury? If the team is deprived of some of those key men who would play 80-90% of games, then perhaps it figures that 'mere squad players' will be switched between in their absence?

Rafa also lost his right-hand man, and while I feel that the club can recover from Pako Ayestaran's departure, and weren't exactly relying on him for every important decision, it was a shock to the system that, at the time, could not have helped. It coincided with the international break that disrupted the great form the Reds were showing, and also coincided with the loss of Agger and Alonso.

More recently, Torres had actually just played three games in a row before he went to Spain with his national team, and without Rafa's careful training regime which staves off a lot of muscle injuries, promptly got injured.

So how can you just blame rotation when there are clearly far more disruptive factors? How do you strip away these crucial factors, any of which on their own could cause problems, to leave you with the all-too-simple conclusion that "I'm afraid it's that rotation system again"?

It's becoming a cliché, but it needs saying: no-one blamed rotation when the Champions League was won and a final reached last season, or when the Reds were winning 10 or 12 games on the trot when reaching 82 league points. But of course, had Liverpool lost just one of those dozen games, despite Rafa making changes each and every week, the lazy hindsight pundits would say "you never change a winning team".

How the hell can Rafa win, then? Damned if he does, damned if he doesn't, by men who always know better after the event.

Does winning the league mean you are the best manager ever, but not winning it, when there are three other very strong rivals — two of whom have spent more on their squads, and two of whose managers have been in their jobs for a combined 33 years — make you a total idiot? And all this, while Liverpool are having the best league start for years, where they remain unbeaten. Points have been dropped, but the situation is hardly bleak, nor will it be even if the Reds lose against Arsenal. (Although it won't help, clearly). There's three-quarters of the season to go.

But given that Rafa has proven since 2001 that he's a supreme winner, I want him to use whatever methods he feels suit him. So I support him, even if I don't understand all of his decisions (just as none of us can understand all of any manager's decisions. It can be hard understanding anyone who knows more than you).

He's the world-class manager. Not me. It's pointless having a world-class manager and not letting him do things his own way. If either he, or the next five or ten managers (assuming they were quality appointments), decided consistent team selections were the way to go, I'd support that too.

Not because I'm a Yes Man, but because it's pointless trying to make a top manager work in a way in which he doesn't believe, or forcing him to adhere to methods that are the antithesis of his philosophy (which will have been studiously developed over time, not constructed on some crazy whim.)

It's like a concert promoter booking the world's most famous singers for a global event, and then asking Frank Sinatra to sing like Kurt Cobain or vice versa. (Okay, so their best days are currently behind them, but you get my point.)

Both were great performers in their own way, but if you'd asked Sinatra to sing 'Smells Like Teen Spirit' to grungy guitars and Cobain to croon 'It Was A Very Good Year', neither would be playing to his strengths. It wouldn't work.

The press, and some fans, have a terrible habit of telling top managers what to do. Often — and this is what riles me — it is not given as an opinion that accepts some humility, as in "I think it might be better...", but as stone cold fact.

Over the years when things weren't going so well, Wenger was told that, in order to succeed again, he needed to toughen up his fancy footballers; to introduce more English players who understand the Premiership; to stop over-passing; to go more direct, and introduce wingers who cross the ball; and so on. Alex Ferguson has been told to be less aggressive and stubborn, to not play kids, as well as instructed who to buy and sell, amongst other things.

These type of comments appear during the lean years, of which both men have had a few. Critics claimed both men had taken things as far as they could.

Over time both men have seen their styles evolve ever so slightly, but neither has eschewed the majority of the supposed "negative" aspects of their methodology or personality. If anything, Arsenal's current success is built on even fewer Englishmen — with Cole and Campbell gone, Wenger has an entirely foreign team most weeks.

These men stick to what works for them — but of course, it can't work every year, and often it doesn't work for years at a time.

Make no mistake: Rafa is being hung out to dry by the media. The man has made errors, but then so too has every manager.

It's become a game of hangman, and I fear he won't win; more than anything, I fear the self-fulfilling prophecy of fans baying for blood. It doesn't help that this bloodlust is being served by men in the media who want to make money by criticising the club we love if there's a story to be had, for institutions that want to make money by criticising the club we love if it suits them.

The pressure is building, and much of it is down to the ludicrous criticism of a system too many people either don't understand, or who close their eyes to the facts. It sure ain't perfect, but what the hell is?

So I rest my case for the defence. It's time to acquit Rafael Benítez, and allow him his freedom: the freedom to make the choices he feels are necessary to get Liverpool back to the top, whether it's this year or a little beyond.

This piece was written two days after the defeat in Turkey against Besiktas. The next results were a 1-1 draw at home to Arsenal, a 2-1 victory against Cardiff in the Carling Cup, and a 0-0 draw at Blackburn in which the Reds shaded the game due a late onslaught but couldn't break through. The issue of rotation was still prevalent.

Then, while under great pressure to get a result, the Reds beat Besiktas 8-0 with a heavily rotated side (four changes). Instead of praise for rotation working, the focus was on whether Benítez would 'stay sane' and keep an unchanged line-up for only the third time in over 150 games for the next match, against Fulham. Unpredictable as ever, he did just that. The Reds dominated the game, but it wasn't until the three late substitutes were on that the screw was turned, and a 2-0 win secured.

Benítez then returned to picking the players he felt were right for each particular game, and the Reds won 3-0 at Newcastle (five changes), 4-1 at home to Porto in another high-pressure must-win clash (four changes), and then 4-0 at home (five changes) to a Bolton team who were fresh from drawing at Bayern Munich in the Uefa Cup and beating Manchester United at home in the league. Suddenly there was no mention of rotation on TV and in the newspapers. Of course, there also wasn't any mention that Liverpool had just won five games in a row, scoring 21 goals, to just one conceded, while making four or five changes in all but one of the matches. It was the perfect example of how rotation is only criticised when the team is under par, but conveniently overlooked when it's playing beautifully.

As soon as Liverpool lost the next game, 3-1 at Reading, the knives were predictably out for Benítez and his rotation policy once more. The Guardian listed the "selections Rafa had got wrong"; nowhere was it mentioned that he'd just seen an inspired run of results from making such changes. Meanwhile, Arsenal dropped five points in four days in the North-east, soon after a European away defeat, but Wenger's selections were not remotely questioned.

Will Liverpool Survive Football's Boom-to-Bust?
October 2001

Football is crumbling. Boom is turning to bust.

Maybe. Maybe not.

Whatever does happen, things are definitely slowing down. Not a day goes past without someone predicting doom and gloom for the sport. Forecasts say the next Premiership TV deal will be for less than the current one. "Football" thought it could expand exponentially, like a kid blowing up a balloon and amazed to see it grow to the size of Norfolk. But that balloon is making some awful creaking sounds, and people in Norwich are running for cover.

David Murray, Chairman of Rangers, has predicted that one major European club will go bankrupt soon. Lazio have downscaled their activities to the point where they will cull many senior members of their squad at the end of the season (offloading them, as opposed to mass slaughter, I assume), and have asked players to take pay cuts in setting a salary cap.

The European game is of course structured differently to ours, and always has been. Italian teams don't tend to own their own stadia, and companies like Fiat (in the case of Juventus) bankroll their best teams. Spanish giants Real Madrid can get into debt to the tune of £200m and still not be in danger of folding; yes, they were lucky enough to be in a position to sell their training ground and clear their debts . . . before instantly going out like a coked-up shopaholic with a new credit card and buying Zinedine Zidane for £50m.

But Real also have a whole host of generous benefactors. Of course, English football has had its Jack Walkers and Sir Jack Haywards and Lionel Pickerings. But these are the exceptions, and Blackburn, Wolves and Derby found that their generous 'uncles' didn't have unlimited resources. All bought big, then sold big soon after. All were either soon relegated to the First Division, or unable to escape it in the first place.

So football may implode. The question I am asking is: When the shit kung-fu kicks the fan, will the Reds come out smelling of roses? Will the club be one of those left standing? Is Liverpool FC in a position of great strength, or built on quicksand?

Someone on a forum recently made the point of questioning the validity of survival, if it's just ourselves and Manchester United who are left standing, like those twin pillars Big Daddy and Giant Haystacks on World of Sport, circa 1984. Aside the obvious benefit of Liverpool finally winning every game during the season, it would of course not be good for the game. But the majority of big clubs will survive any fall out; however, it's the shape they are in on the other side that will be the point of interest. And if, due to sound financial planning, Liverpool are one of only a handful of healthy clubs, is that our problem? It will be sad, but not as sad as biting the dust.

Yes, we want healthy competition for our team, but throughout the ages clubs have had to manage their resources in the most sensible manner. Is it our fault Everton are in a financial mess? Little over a decade ago they were in the supposed Big Five. Now they nowhere near it. You could end up with the Scottish situation of two super-powers and a plethora of powder puffs, but if so, I'd rather be the equivalent of Rangers or Celtic than Aberdeen or Dundee. It might get boring winning the league ten years in succession, but that's the kind of boredom I'd like to test-drive, thank you very much. I mean, it just sounds *awful*, doesn't it? — pipping Manchester United for the title for a straight decade.

The Champions League is where the money is at, and has become the obsession of Europe's bigger teams, to the point where you have the G14 (including Liverpool) 'perhaps' looking to say 'to hell' with all this qualification lark, we'll have our own regular league where we can all get fatter as the rest grow weak and wither. But until the G14 (or G237 as it will no doubt eventually become, to make sure the Faroe Islands can be sold TV rights of a competition including their top three sides) actually does anything, the Champions League is the place to be seen.

What's our future Champions League outlook? Do we deserve to be in the last sixteen of the Champions League? Are we deservedly ranked twelfth in Europe, or is it a false position? Can our future be at least iridescently bright, if eternal success cannot be totally assured?

In less than a year we have accrued *ten* competitive victories (i.e. not pre-season friendlies but including the Charity Shield and European Super Cup) against sides from this year's last sixteen: the 'elite'. And only one defeat. We have beaten Manchester United *four* times (in just ten and a half months), Arsenal twice (with an aggregate score of 6-1), Barcelona, Roma (away) and Porto, as well as a win against last year's Champions of Europe, Bayern Munich. Ten wins, two draws, one defeat, and of those ten wins only one (Arsenal in the FA Cup Final) was in any way fortuitous. To me, that's the form of the best side in Europe; I'm not saying we are, of course (heaven forbid), but a more daring man than I could make such a bold statement and try to make it stick. Five trophies in six months might get bandied about as well, just to bolster the argument.

To think that we are still only halfway towards our goal of 'plan completion', estimated at another two or three years' time, when Owen, Gerrard, Heskey, Carragher, Murphy, *et al*, will be more experienced, and when other talented youngsters will be knocking at the door with their youthful enthusiasm. We are halfway there, but in danger of cocking things up by going ahead and winning the big trophies before schedule. However, even if we don't win anything this year, the progress is there for all to see. In fact, the future is almost visible, in the form of the wonderful squad Gérard Houllier has assembled. It would be a great thing to fast-forward into the future to see what becomes of that talent.

[*Okay, here I am! — and clearly not enough came of that talent. Given that the piece was written in 2001, it has to be noted that it really was a very good squad at the time, if perhaps not wonderful. Markus Babbel was still very much part of the picture, before illness took its toll, as were talented technical footballers like Litmanen, McAllister, Berger, Fowler and Ziege, none of whom lasted more than another year at the club. And at the time Sinama-Pongolle and Le Tallec, signed as 16-year-olds, seemed to have the world at their feet, as did Gregory Vignal. This was before Houllier dismantled a large part of the squad and replaced those stars with inferior additions, and before the youngsters failed to develop as expected.*]

The foundations at Liverpool are looking firm, hence the optimism. It's not just the first team, it's the whole set up — the players, the reserves, the youth team starlets, the management and the ever-more impressive coaching staff. Even the tea lady can be trusted to take training from time to time, although she's had to readjust her thinking from wingbacks to a flat back four since Houllier arrived, and prefers two up front as opposed to 'split' strikers. The Academy is the best facility in Europe, and a new state-of-the-art training complex is being built to replace Melwood. So far so good.

So the foundations are in place. Chelsea also put down some really solid, concrete foundations; unfortunately, it was for a luxury hotel. They seemed to forget about an ageing team. Two years ago they undertook their future financial planning with the City, and arrogantly (or just plain stupidly) based all their calculations on being in the Champions League in the next few seasons. In the last two seasons they have not been in the Champions League, and went out of the UEFA Cup at the first hurdle against minnows both times, at a potential cost of around £10m a season. Clubs like Chelsea will survive, but suffer in terms of the teams they can field. Their lack of intelligent long-term planning could do them massive damage. Marcel Desailly may have to retire, and Zola is on his last legs. John Terry aside, where's the real top class young talent coming through? Yes, there are one or two young other players of merit, but nowhere near as many as clubs such as ourselves, Manchester United and Leeds. [*We don't need reminding that it took a Russian billionaire to bail them out . . .*]

I could name an entire team of brilliant 21-year-olds or younger at Anfield (including not yet arrived but already signed Milan Baros, Florent Sinama-Pongolle and Anthony Le Tallec), the majority of whom are as good in their age group as anyone in the world; some (Gerrard and Owen) are almost as good as the very best players of any age in the world. As well as Baros, Simana-Pongolle and Le Tallec you have Chris Kirkland, Stephen Wright, Gregory Vignal, Djimi Traore, Michael Owen, John Arne Riise, Steven Gerrard, John Welsh, Richie Partridge, Daniel Sjolund and others like Neil Mellor, who are only now starting to make waves for the youth team and reserves. [*How average too many of them turned out to be.*] Behind these you have David Raven, singled out for a special award as being one of the four best players in his age group (sixteen) in the country. Raven, Welsh, Simana-Pongolle and Le Tallec are either only sixteen, or very recently turned seventeen.

But the future isn't just down to the extremely youthful. Players in their mid-twenties (three years either side of 25) include: Danny Murphy, Patrik Berger, Robbie Fowler, Vladimir Smicer, Emile Heskey, Jamie Carragher, Jerzy Dudek, Veggard Heggem, Bernard Diomede, Didi Hamann, Stephane Henchoz, Nick Barmby, Jamie Redknapp, Igor Biscan and Sami Hyypia. If Gary McAllister is anything to go by, those players have up to a maximum of another decade in the top flight, but even the eldest should manage six years as a minimum. [*On average, those players managed another three years at Anfield, although most were still in top-flight football five years later.*] Not all will be at Liverpool in six years' time; but all could be. Only Jari Litmanen and Gary McAllister are currently in their 30s, and the Finn barely so.

The mix is also roughly 50-50, split between English and foreign; a nice blend between the different skills and attributes homegrown and continental players offer. There's an excellent balance to the whole set up. This has been planned; it isn't by accident. Houllier knows English talent is overpriced, but it hasn't stopped him buying Heskey, Barmby and Kirkland. Unfortunately those three cost in excess of £25m, so English purchases have been scarcer than foreign buys; fortunately there were enough youth team graduates about the place to more than compensate.

The predicted downturn for the game in general does put a question mark on the wisdom of Liverpool building a new stadium, hence Rick Parry's recent statements about checking whether it's financially viable first, before jumping headfirst into such a massive undertaking. Maybe this was just 'paper talk' to pacify the brilliantly organised Anfield4Ever group, after they petitioned him over the summer. Maybe the club will go ahead regardless. But even in the month or two since that statement, the downturn has gathered pace. Since the summer we've had terrorism on a grand scale, and a new kind of war. All this at a time when worldwide recession was forecast. (Excuse my ignorance, but where does all the money go in a *worldwide* recession?) Too many teams have sacrificed squad building for Stadia building — to get more money by having more fans inside the ground, but then finding themselves with half-empty stadiums in the First Division.

Liverpool were recently held up as a club in trouble, as the percentage of its wages-to-turnover was the highest around, and that, as a result, the club was losing money. The wage bill was around 75% of Liverpool's turnover for the season 1999/2000. But that was the Great Season of Rebuilding, with essential purchases made and wages rising as a result. The club bought ten players that season, for around £40 million, including £8m on Hamann and £11m on Heskey. Also, the Reds went out of all cups at the first hurdle, and unlike Chelsea, weren't even in the Uefa Cup to fall at the first. That clearly affected turnover. It was not a good season in itself — better in that the foundations were laid at that point.

This year the Reds have an already guaranteed £20m from the Champions League (it all seemed so easy), but of course that can all go wrong in subsequent years — hence the importance of those foundations. All the same, it was encouraging to make almost £20m from the three cups last year, proving that the Champions League isn't the be-all-and-end-all. There are other ways to make money, and not all of them involve fleecing the fans. Liverpool also made £18m from the Premiership, as part of the new TV deal. The deal is broken down into three parts: an equal share all clubs get, of around £6.3m; a merit share, which was again around £6m as a reward for coming third in the league, with only Arsenal and Manchester United receiving more, obviously; and the final third, made up from TV appearance bonus money — only United received more from this, as the two most televised teams, which befits the status as the two most supported clubs.

There was also a new Reebok deal, a £20m internet broadband broadcasting rights deal, and the money from the league attendances — through the turnstiles, as they used to say. Rick Parry may not be everyone's cup of tea, but at least he seems to have a firm grasp of the realities of the game. (Yes, he was partly responsible for the whole 1990s football 'boom', having negotiated the Sky contract on behalf of the Premiership, but surely his remit was to get as much money out of the suits beneath Murdoch's wing as possible? Sky were always going to charge fans a lot of money to watch, so they may as well have been paying good money themselves. Yes, he was partly responsible for setting up the Premier League, but this was something that would have happened at that stage anyway.)

The latest Sky TV contract is ludicrously large, and ITV paid a hell of a lot of money for highlights, only to find people preferred to watch Blind

Date (who are these people? Admittedly Blind Date is only marginally more cringeworthy than Des Lynam and Terry Venables trying to be comedians in between Andy Townsend stating things like "Michael Owen — he's fast, y'know? If he gets in behind you, you know what? — he'll punish you" in the back of a dustcart, but Blind Date? And I wanted to give the great British public some credit.)

Football audiences have been on the wane for some time now. Last season's FA Cup final was the most exciting prospect in years (turned out to be quite exciting, too), but only five million people tuned in. Years ago, before the boom, up to 20 million people would regularly gather around the box. Not only are Liverpool and Arsenal massively supported clubs, but it was one for the neutrals, too. Okay, it just happened to coincide with the hottest day in the capital since the Great Fire of London, but is a bit of warmth really enough of an excuse to not watch the domestic calender's greatest showcase?

Does it highlight how fickle the majority of football watchers actually are? Was it a case of overkill, at the end of a TV football-saturated season, or proof that not that many people actually care that deeply about the game? When England managed 25 million viewers for the Argentina game in 1998, how many of those were *bona fide* football fans, or football 'haters' (you know them, they watch Blind Date) carried along for the ride; unable to resist the flow, simply joining in down the pub as it's better than being home alone? — in the way I hate watching tennis, but can just about get interested enough to watch the Wimbledon final.

Now we have ITV Digital, having negotiated a £300m deal with the Football League, looking to 'renegotiate' that sum three months into the first season of the deal's existence. "It's far too much", the broadcaster is now saying. It makes you wonder if someone might have thought about that before signing on the dotted line. One First Division game they were showing (the £300m breaks down to a cost of around £1.2m per match) attracted a measly 1,000 viewers — the average attendance of a less-well supported Vauxhaul Conference side. A newspaper worked out that it would have been cheaper for ITV Digital to have chauffeur-driven each individual to the match, put them all up for a night in a five star hotel, and still had enough left over to be able to give them each £500 spending money. If 1,000 tune in for a First Division match, it makes you wonder how many pay-per-viewers ITV Digital get for their football league PPV subscription games like Kidderminster vs Macclesfield. People don't even watch the Champions League on ITV Digital (the biggest audience is around 88,000 for the Reds' home game against Boavista, although apparently only 4,000 saw the Dortmund home game), so ITV1 have finally been granted permission from Uefa to show the game with Barcelona live on a Tuesday, followed by the usual Wednesday offering of Manchester United, although in this case at least they are playing decent opposition in Bayern Munich. ITV Digital claim to be the only channel showing all the live games of United, Arsenal and Liverpool, and true as that might be, it doesn't help that most people already have Sky installed. ITV Digital are now thinking of offering the Champions League to Sky subscribers, as a mark of desperation.

Sky started showing football a decade ago, so most football fans invested in Sky; they then introduced extra Sports channels for different competitions, so that England matches or the League Cup or pre-season friendlies would be on channels that at other times will only show International Tiddlywinks and the European Over 80s Croquet Finals. So you finally subscribe to all three channels, and they go all 'digital' — the channel where they hide away the Uefa Cup games they snaffle up.

I was foolish enough to invest in Ondigital (now ITV Digital) two years ago. I get the Sky Sport channels, but not the Sky Digital channels. I decided to hang on to the box in the hope that the Reds would finally get into the Champions League, and after one calamitous cock-up, they finally made it. Still, I'd be able to take advantage of ITV Digital's free Champs League coverage.

Wrong. It would now cost £6 a month for those games.

The League Cup's demise is part of the overkill of the game. The cup (now on ITV Digital — don't they just have the midas touch?) has been devalued because clubs no longer field their strongest teams, and as a spectacle it now rates low on fans' agendas. Harsh on the competition, maybe, but it's a fact of life. In the mid-80s, seeing a League Cup game on TV was a big deal; now you can see 101 games on TV each week — hell, each *evening* — ranging from domestic, to European, South American, Brazilian Beach, Irish Beach (yes, it happened), to over-35s Masters, Soap Stars Five-a-Side, and C-List Celebrities Underwater Headers and Volleys. Finding a decent match to watch — now that's a different matter. Going to see a League Cup game ends up being too expensive with the price of a football match going through the roof. Of course, being the weakest link in the football trophy chain, it had to suffer most. The League Cup has always been a poor relation of the FA Cup: virtually the same thing — just without the non-league clubs and the extra 100 years of wonderful history behind it. Other competitions are seeing attendances dwindle, but the League Cup is feeling the strain most.

If managers think that we play too much football these days then they must prioritise, and as the lowest valued prize, the League Cup suffers. It's natural wastage. Manchester United use it to blood youth team players, and in a bizarre way it would take something like their youth team winning it to raise the stakes again. Then it could almost become a glorified youth team cup, where the Premiership's youth teams take on the rest of the lower leagues — doesn't that sound like a fair challenge? It could be quite fascinating. Maybe it needs that kind of twist to breathe some life back into it. Otherwise it will continue to slowly atrophy.

But in general the quality of football in this country remains high. The 'product' is good. But it's like Mars bars: there is a limit to the amount you can stomach, even if, like me, you consider them manna from heaven. (Any more than seven for breakfast, however, and I'm vomiting.)

So what happens next is anyone's guess. Boom to bust, or miraculous bust-back-to-boom? We'll all continue supporting Liverpool, but whether football will be the same is a mystery. Sometimes I look at those old guys in the ground — the men who look like they're in their 70s or 80s — and think: do you understand what's going on? Not in a patronising way — just that football today is not the game they must have fallen in love with. Football in the third Millennia is not like the old days. The pace faster; the money astronomically greater; the rules changed to the point where even the players and referees don't seem to know them — referees and lines-'people' are asked to use their common sense and then reprimanded when they do so; the ball lightened and lightened until it weighs little more than a baby sparrow and wobbles in the air like one of those crappy balls you get for 50p from the petrol garage, complete with the fake painted hexagons; the kits altered as if *haute couture*; the language worse; the refs verbally and physically abused; the players diving and cheating; the celebrations changed from a simple manly pat on the back and a "well done Smithers" to simulations of full-blown sex; and — most miraculously — the goalies actually capable of saving the ball instead of just falling down three seconds after it hits the back of the net (before throwing a resigned look from under a cloth cap).

I look at these old fellas, and think: If they are here now, I'll be sitting here in fifty years' time. You bet your bottom dollar. I just hope Liverpool Football Club is there, too. Otherwise I'll feel a right prick sitting in Anfield if the club moved to Stanley Park forty-five years earlier . . .

Interesting that Leeds imploded fairly quickly after this article appeared. As did ITV Digital, and not long after that, ITV's The Premiership disappeared, along with its infamous tactics truck.

What would I do differently to Rafa?

October 2007

I was recently challenged to suggest what I disagreed with about Rafa Benítez's management. This happened to come a couple of weeks after a liverpoolfc. tv piece where I tried to explain how difficult it is to pinpoint a manager's mistakes with any certainty.

Perhaps that message didn't get through. If a goalkeeper drops the ball, it's a mistake. It's easy to spot. The same with a striker missing an open goal. But managerial mistakes are a much more complex issue.

At times there can be plenty I wish Rafa did differently, but that doesn't mean that he was wrong and my ideas would have worked out better. I always have the advantage of hindsight, as well as my ideas ending (in my head at least) in perfection; as if that would be the reality.

Based on his showing against Charlton, I was certain Kewell should have started in the Champions League final last year, but when he did come on it showed that he still lacked match sharpness. This is something only a manager can know for sure. I'd also have brought on Crouch earlier, but at 1-0 it was delicately balanced, and maybe Rafa didn't want the players being tempted to hit long balls. Had that happened, he'd have been slated.

These are two quick examples of why I think it's nigh-on impossible to judge what constitutes a managerial error.

On any given day, did the team lose because the strikers didn't take their chances? The defenders marked badly, or other examples of human error? Because of bad tactics? An outrageously good piece of 'unstoppable' play from the opposition, or an inspired display as they raise their game? Bad refereeing decisions? Poor motivation from the manager and his staff? A lack of preparation time? The players just weren't good enough on the day, or some are not good enough, full stop? The opposition had a midweek off while your team schlepped across Europe?

Or could it be an impossibly complex mix of some or all of these reasons and many more, with a precise single reason impossible to pinpoint? With this in mind, I tend to try and judge a manager over a period of time, because then patterns emerge.

The manager takes the overall responsibility. But he can't control everything.

Cause and effect makes it virtually impossible to judge things like substitutions; you never get to compare the alternative situations, where the change is not made, or another player is introduced instead. And of course, a manager is one step removed from the action. He sends on a player, but he doesn't play for him.

If a manager makes a substitution, he is relying on that human being to not make mistakes on his behalf. Arguably a good manager will choose the right players more often than not: those least likely to make a mistake, and most likely to do something positive.

But in any given player can err at any unexpected moment. I'm sure when Martin O'Neill sent on Marlon Harewood in a like-for-like swap with his team 4-1 up at Spurs (a decision that made sense to me at the time) he didn't expect his striker to give away a totally needless penalty that swung the game in Spurs' favour; the game took on a life-force of its own, and ended 4-4.

Benítez's most lauded substitution mirrors his predecessor's most criticised, in that both involved Didi Hamann in a crucial Champions League match, with the club as close to winning the trophy as it had been since its days as the European Cup. Houllier took off Hamann; Benítez put him on.

Houllier took off Hamann when the team were losing 3-2 but winning on the away goals rule, and in desperate need of keep Bayer Leverkusen out, while Benítez put him on when the team was 3-0 down and needed to score at least three goals.

Neither substitution therefore makes a lot of sense in terms of the personnel involved. It was the opposite action in terms of logic — you want Hamann on to protect a lead, but he wouldn't be the first choice to overturn a massive deficit.

In fairness to Houllier, Hamann wasn't having much of an effect against Leverkusen before being taken off. Had he stayed on, the way the game was going, and given how he was being overrun, then it's still likely Liverpool would have lost. As strange as the decision still seems to this day, it's not as if the Reds were in control and no gamble was needed.

And where Benítez got lucky was Milan's failure to score from one of their early second-half chances (which Hamann did nothing to prevent) which stopped the Italians from completely killing off his team's hopes.

Where the switch deserves praise was was in the move from a back four to a three, and in how Hamann's presence freed up Gerrard to attack. Benítez's luck doubled when Smicer, only on the field as the manager's gamble with Kewell had failed, scored with the kind of moment of supreme inspiration sadly lacking during most of the Czech's appearances.

Benítez then earned his corn by switching Gerrard to right-back, to cope with Serginho's surges. But it still required Djimi Traoré — who was due to be removed at half-time — to produce a goal-line clearance to keep the Reds' hopes alive. So while part of Benítez's success that night was in making masterful tactical changes, it also required good luck and bad finishing from the opposition (Shevchenko in particular) to have them pay off.

It's fair to say that I often disagree with Rafa's team selections/rotations on a match-by-match basis, but the overall pattern is one I cannot argue too much with. And after all, that is the point of rotation. I trust that he has much more information to hand, on both the opposition and his own players, not to mention a far greater knowledge of the game.

Aside from Harry Kewell, whose injury problems pre-date Benítez's arrival, few of his players have suffered from serious muscle injuries. The manager has had less fortune with the unavoidable loss of players to broken bones. The Reds have ended each season well; that may not all be down to rotation, but at the same time, it doesn't mean early defeats are, too.

Patterns are what I tend to look at when assessing a manager, because they show a long-term picture, not merely what is happening in the moment, be it a bad defeat or healthy win. Managers who make too many mistakes do not have good records. But even the best managers have bad months, even bad seasons. But look at their five-season records, and the best stand out as a class above.

While not all the patterns in Rafa's reign make good viewing (autumnal slumps, overall away form, league goals scored), the overall picture remains pretty impressive.

Countering the autumnal slumps are the runs of wins his teams always put together, although of course the eradication of the former would go a long way towards a league title. The home form is a slight concern this season, although Rafa's overall record at Anfield is very impressive; the away form, meanwhile, has actually been excellent in alternate years, just dire every second season. Overall it averages out at merely average, but the chance is there this season to improve that.

Regarding league goalscoring, this is the first season when Rafa's had a strikeforce he's close to being entirely happy with, and it has 15 goals to its name already, with seven in the league. While the latter figure is not amazing, it is currently better than the league goals from the strikers at United (five) or Chelsea (two), who have played one more game.

Of course, it would help if Steven Gerrard was weighing in with his share, as he's capable of doing, and in the way Cesc Fabregas currently is at Arsenal.

Rafa's record in the Premiership since he arrived gives him a 54% win-rate. This despite two end of seasons where, for acceptable reasons, he fielded weakened teams in the league to save the players for the more crucial Champions League games. While his win-rate has been slipping since 2006, it's too soon to read too much into this season; at the same point in the last two seasons it was also poor at this stage, only to recover considerably.

To put it into a kind of context, the Reds won three league titles with identical or lower win-rates, plus another five with only marginally better win-rates. And his total of 54% is considerably weakened by his first season, which was a steep learning curve for all concerned (as was Bill Shankly's). Rafa's Premiership win record excluding that first season is nearing 60%.

The trouble since his arrival, and which would make the job more difficult for anybody, is that teams have needed to win more than 70% of matches to land the title, something Liverpool have only done once in their illustrious history (71% in 1979). Rafa's best is the 66% from 2005/06, which is the still the second-highest ever.

Rafa's overall record in all competitions is even more impressive, at 59%, with 111 wins from 188 games. This contains a disproportionate amount of cup games against Chelsea, plus opposition that includes AC Milan, Juventus, Manchester United and Barcelona.

It's worth mentioning that even now, into his fourth season, he has yet to face a side in the any domestic cup who were below mid-table in the Championship at the time, while the 2006 FA Cup success was based on beating Premiership opposition; only Luton were in a lower division.

The Champions League qualifiers have grown increasingly more difficult (on paper at least) each season. That said, games like TNS were a 'gimme'.

Rafa's record in Europe is second to none since 2004. Not only has he qualified for the competition every season — something that wasn't happening prior to his arrival, and not at all during the '90s — the Reds have also emerged from the group stage in three successive seasons. That impressive record is in danger of falling this season, but there's still plenty of time to turn it around.

The pattern regarding clean sheets is superb: every season Pepe Reina seems to break another record or pass a milestone, and for two seasons running he has racked up the most shut-outs.

The pattern of defending set-pieces is also excellent; however, the pattern of scoring them is less impressive. It's been better than a lot of Reds realise, as fans are always acutely aware of how many corners fail to lead to goals (something not noticed with the other teams, when you often just see the goals they score in highlights), but it still falls a long way short of Chelsea's set-piece success.

On balance, Rafa's record in the transfer market is also impressive. All managers end up getting a fair few wrong (I can name 20-30 flops of Arsene Wenger), but Rafa's generally got his money back (or even made a profit) on his flops, none of whom have been expensive. Unlike some managers, he's also been quick to offload those who don't meet his standards.

It's too early to judge this year's crop, but Torres looks as if he should prove a bargain even at £20m, while Voronin has thus far been excellent value as a free transfer. There have been good signs from the others, but the jury is understandably still out.

And the only reason people might now suggest that signings like Kuyt or Crouch are failures — when in the past they've looked like successes — is because their chances are being limited by the arrival of an even better player. Similarly, the talented but inconsistent Sissoko will struggle to get regular games because of better players Benítez has bought in his position; even so, the Malian remains an important squad member.

Few managers have bought 'spine' players who are better than Reina, Agger, Alonso, Mascherano and Torres.

Even now, the oldest, Alonso, is only 25. These are players yet to enter their prime. (On his good days, Sissoko also looks like he belongs in this company, but he needs to cut out those very bad days.) You can add Scott Carson to the list, but his value may be in the transfer fee it brings, which could be ten-twelve times the £750,000 Benítez paid. Aston Villa have already paid £2m just to take him on loan for a year.

Rafa's had less success on the flanks, although Arbeloa looks a real find, and Ryan Babel has the potential to be a world-class attacking player in any position. But at 20 he's still raw, and needs to toughen up a bit, like a lot of newcomers to English football.

Jermaine Pennant is still only halfway to being a great player — a lot of his game is there, but the lack of goals is a concern. Leto has talent, but is still very raw. Gonzalez flattered to deceive, while Nunez was an inexpensive gamble that didn't pay off. Yossi Benayoun has the ability to buck the trend, and unlike Pennant, can score as well as create.

Meanwhile, in what I believe is much of his best work (but which is still in its infancy), Benítez has totally overhauled the youth and reserve teams, and done so with superb vision.

Like a man planting acorns, it takes a while to see mighty oaks grow. Only a few can manifest — there's not room for them all, after all — but Hobbs and Insua look very much like future stars who are growing ever closer to the first team picture. And of course, the Brazilian Lucas has a massive future in the game.

Do I like the tactics Rafa deploys and the football the Reds play? Generally, yes.

When the team is playing to the level of which it's capable, I have no real complaints about anything, even if the football, while attractive and based around pass and move, doesn't reach the aesthetic excellence of Arsenal's best. When Liverpool are on form, the ball is passed very well, and the movement is top-class. The 2007 Champions League Final was an example of this; all that was lacking was the pace of a top-class striker like Torres.

But of course, when the team is playing badly and its confidence is low, a number of faults appear. This is the same with any team, though. Not enough players show for the ball; the play can get narrow; the defenders look long; individual mistakes creep in. But these are often failings of the team's psychology at that moment in time, not of any tactical instruction.

If you look at Benítez's purchases, they are almost all technically excellent. In particular, it's a shame for Peter Crouch that his sublime control is under-appreciated by many observers, and his aerial game obsessed over. Even Sissoko often shows great control and twinkle toes when in possession, but his concentration when passing lets him down.

I get the impression that Benítez wants his team to always play attractive passing football, and be clever and creative in the final third, but that it's not always possible. He also wants the team to be compact, and to play 'as one'. Earlier in the season this was happening, and the Reds looked a real force. Beyond confidence, there's nothing to stop it happening again.

So as for what I'd do differently, there's plenty. But it's almost certain that Liverpool would be a worse team because of it.

Why Liverpool Will Win The Champions League
March 11, 2005

And then there were eight. Finally, and with some sense of disbelief, talk is starting to turn to Liverpool actually winning the Champions League — no one necessarily expecting it, but offering a case of *why not?*

Why not indeed? I certainly don't think there's less talent at Liverpool than there was at Porto last season. I don't think the club has an inferior manager, either. A bit of long-overdue luck, and who knows?

"The best teams don't always win the Champions League," Jamie Carragher said following with win against Bayer Leverkusen, with more than a degree of truth — and Liverpool are certainly not the best team in Europe right now. Not even close.

However, it is equally true that to win it more than once, and in quick succession (four times in eight seasons, as an example — and a completely random one, of course), is definitive proof you're the best. You can get lucky once, perhaps — favourable draw, fortunate decisions, no injuries (and Alex Ferguson noted how fortunate United were on that score in 1999 — not one major casualty). But the most accurate marker of greatness is consistency. Because even the flukiest team on earth cannot ride their luck indefinitely. Going back and doing it again, and again, and again, is what counts. 'One-offs' are great, but to become legendary takes more. Why do you think Ferguson couldn't retire a couple of years back, as previously planned? Because he knew that whatever people's opinions on who was the greatest, the record books show: Bob Paisley, European Cup Winner three times in nine years; Alex Ferguson, winner just once in twenty.

At this stage of the team's development under Benitez, doing so just once after a 21-year wait would be truly astonishing. It seems almost surreal to be contemplating it. (And I'm still not sure I'm actually contemplating it, or just contemplating the thought of contemplating it).

When Liverpool reached the Quarter Finals in 2002, it was directly following the Treble, and with the side challenging Arsenal for that season's Premiership title. The club was riding the crest of a wave, and it came as no great surprise to get that far. The surprise was that it ended how it did.

The mood of the fans leaving the Bay Arena two nights ago could not have been more in contrast with three years earlier. Again Bayer scored a late goal, but this time it was utterly meaningless. Rafa, fresh from getting the ales in, even had time to make a nod towards the defeat three years ago, by mirroring Houllier's withdrawal of Didi Hamann — arguably the most famous removal of a player in the club's history (its recent history, at least). This time it was with the job done, to save the German from picking up a suspension.

Many of the broadsheets opted for the angle that on Wednesday night Liverpool met an incredibly poor German side, shorn of several key players. (Interestingly, many ignored the fact that Liverpool had a far longer list of absentees, with far more quality in their ranks of wounded and ineligible.) Bayer were a side who had already beaten Bayern Munich 4-1 at home in the Bundesliga, and scored three goals in demolishing each of Real Madrid, Roma and Dynamo Kiev on their way to topping the 'Group of Death'.

Suddenly they were whipping boys, simply because we whipped them.

Benitez has led his threadbare collection of fit players to a stage in the competition where, after next week's delayed game between Inter and Porto, only seven other teams will remain. While no one will retain any credibility by suggesting the Reds are now a better side than Manchester United, Arsenal, Real Madrid, Barcelona and all the other top sides to have fallen before the Quarter Finals, the fact remains that they are all out, and the Reds are in the hat on Friday week. Liverpool may have had a slightly easier draw, but there was nothing lucky about the way the team performed over the two legs. Leverkusen's home record has been remarkable. There had to be a reason for that.

To put the win against Leverkusen into perspective, an entire team of players — goalkeeper, defenders, midfielders and strikers — were missing and, given there were no suspensions, it was either through injury or ineligibility.

Look at the list: Kirkland, Josemi, Pellegrino, Traore, Alonso, Kewell, Sinama-Pongolle, Mellor, Cissé and Morientes. (Okay, so it's a ten-man team). How many of those would have been in the 18-man squad — the starting XI and seven subs allowed in Europe — if they had been available to Rafa? Almost certainly all, with the possible exception of Mellor. Of the 18 Rafa did select, only half would have been certainties: Dudek, Carragher, Finnan, Hyypia, Riise, Gerrard, Hamann, Baros and Luis Garcia. So we were literally at half-strength, in terms of the matchday squad at least.

Given the impressive Biscan (again enjoying a match in Europe) and Warnock (his best game for the club) would not be guaranteed a place in a European 18 if everyone was fit and eligible — not to mention Smicer, Carson, Le Tallec, Mellor, and Nunez — it goes to show that there is still a lot of quality and depth to the Liverpool squad, even if the side could use a couple more 'outstanding' first team players, and some of the squad players are playing for their futures. It also highlights how Benitez has never had the chance to select from anything remotely approaching his full squad. He won't yet know what his best side is, as he's not had the chance to select it.

So while we're clearly still lacking the kind of consistency top clubs need, the performance in Germany showcased the quality the team can produce. Consistency will take time, not to mention the manager being able to pick his best players — or at least able to hit upon a fairly settled side. But it's great to know that our highs can be so high — as some teams just can't play the kind of football we displayed against Leverkusen. And it was no accident, either — while we've been poor too often for anyone's liking, there have also been plenty of scintillating displays. The highs have been stellar.

Fighting on three fronts with only half a squad has taken its toll on our league performances. But it will stand the club in good stead, as fringe players have emerged from the shadows. Where Benitez hasn't had the luxury of learning what his best team is, he has had the chance to find out how good his reserves are.

Much has been made of the financial rewards of qualifying for next season's Champions League, but in exceeding expectations this season the club will have earned more than it planned for — so missing out wouldn't be quite as disastrous in those terms. (Better to have one successful season than

two poor-to-average ones — after all, finishing 3rd and 4th can still mean
Uefa Cup football if you lose the two-leg qualifying tie in August. You'll make
pittance.)

Having said that, qualification remains a massive priority as a) the current
players want to be there, b) it helps attract new players, and c) the club wants to
be challenging for the top trophies. But even if qualification proves a bridge too
far for a squad shorn of half of its senior pros, reaching the last eight helps repair
some of the damage to the club's reputation over recent seasons, and helps put
money in the coffers — never a pleasant thing to concentrate on, but even the
old school of fans know that it's better to have money than to lack it.

Pressure

The role of underdogs could be one that suits the Reds. Last year's Champions
League is a case in point. There was Porto, and there was Monaco. (And two
months later, there was Greece at Euro 2004.) But the example I am thinking
of relates to London.

A strange thing happened when Arsenal met Chelsea. The west London
club had bought their way to their best domestic season for 50 years, but
Arsenal were having a remarkable year, and everyone felt that, for all their
domestic domination, the impressive team Wenger had assembled had to win
the European Cup for any of it to mean anything significant. Victory — moral
victory — belonged to Arsenal before the game kicked off, as everyone knew
they were the better team. Justice needed to be done.

It wasn't that people felt that they would beat Chelsea — although the
bookmakers' odds were incredible — but that they deserved it, on the grounds
of being (as they were then seen) the Greatest Side in the World, Ever™. Also,
that team will have had a sense of 'it's now or never' — they must have known
themselves that they could never play as well again. The hype, and the need to
prove they were as good as they then appeared to be, swallowed them whole
in the second leg.

Arsenal became too desperate for that success, inasmuch as they took all
the pressure onboard and allowed it to suffocate them. It is like this: you are
going for a job interview, for a once-in-a-lifetime position you simply must get
— in fact, your professional reputation rests on it. Fail, and questions will be
asked, no matter that everyone knows you are the best candidate for the job.
Nervous as you sit and shuffle in the waiting room (in the case of a football
match, the tunnel), with palms sweating, heart palpitating, and the colour
draining from your face, you look across and see your rival for the job with a
big smile — the picture of insouciance as they start to whistle a happy tune.
He or she doesn't need the job, and is not expected to get it. And as a result,

they will be able to give the best account of themselves. You know then that you're in trouble.

It happened to Liverpool in 1988. In that case it was the FA Cup final, to complete the double for the second time in three seasons. So stunning had been the team's season up to that point — the football breathtaking, with the attacking play taken to a new level by the arrival of Barnes, Beardsley, Houghton and Aldridge — that it would be the only fitting conclusion.

Liverpool became such overwhelming favourites — unbeatable, people suggested — that Wimbledon, who were then a top-six side, were suddenly regarded by all and sundry as the non-league team they had been in the 1970s. Wimbledon won a large part of that match in the tunnel, before the game. You can call it mind games (the current vogue term), but it's just a simple psyching-out of your opponents. They showed they were 'up for it', and not overawed. And in doing so, they heaped more pressure on the superior team.

Return to the 2003/04 Champions League Quarter Final. Chelsea were allowed to treat the occasion as though they were a non-league side there for a nice day out. Yes, they'd paid £200m to get there, but somehow — and I still don't fully understand quite how they were allowed to get away with it (although part of it was down to the incredible hoodoo Arsenal had over them) — they could ignore that immense expenditure, and pretend they'd exceeded all their hopes and ambitions already. What were in fact two fairly evenly-matched sides, while acknowledging Arsenal's slight superiority, suddenly became David vs Goliath. Once the stakes get so implausibly high for one side, while remaining relatively low for the other, there's trouble for the favourite. They are on a hiding to nothing.

Pressure and expectation affect everything in football. Having won the tie, Chelsea were then favourites to beat Monaco, and as such, were soundly beaten. Pressure can cripple and petrify. I'd suggest that football is down to talent, unity, mentality and fitness. Mentality can often be the most crucial.

The very best players can often deal with pressure, rise above it. But it only takes a few to succumb, and there's trouble. And it's not something that necessarily gets better with age and experience. In his final years as a Liverpool player, Alan Hansen had become not only the team captain but, with Dalglish and Souness no longer in the side, its senior pro. Suddenly there was an extra burden of responsibility, and he felt violently sick before each match, to the point where he hated playing. This was a legend who had played in four European Cup finals, but suddenly a league game at Plough Lane, or The Dell, was making his stomach do cartwheels. That is pressure — and the kind of pressure a player's mind brings to bear on itself. Not just external pressure, but internal pressure. We've seen it with Steven Gerrard in recent weeks.

If we were to face Chelsea in the next round, I would be almost certain of victory — as strange as that might seem. Because no one would give us a cat in hell's chance. Just as last season Chelsea had lost to Arsenal twice in the league, and also in a domestic cup, we've been beaten three times by Mourinho's men already.

But they will be the ones desperate to get through. They will have the expressionless face of a Russian billionaire staring down at them, and maybe the players will read too much into his neutral demeanour and his posse of stony-faced henchmen, and start worrying about those suspicious, capacious vats of cement, and some new supporting columns planned for the Hammersmith flyover.

Sometimes it's easier to 'try hard' when you feel uninhibited, and don't care too much. Sometimes the pressure of having to try *too* hard results in the feeling of running though the aforementioned concrete, when it's half-set — and you look like you're not trying at all. Numb with fear of failure, the game passes you by.

There was a lot of pressure on Liverpool in the recent Carling Cup final in Cardiff, as it was seen as the club's best chance of silverware, and something to rescue a season that was in danger of being railroaded by Everton. Chelsea had bigger fish to fry, and could point to a comfortable lead at the top of the table — why should they be worried about winning the Carling Cup when the bookies had already stopped taking bets on them being English champions? Surely that 'worthless' trophy was the preserve of modern Liverpool? They were still under pressure, to get that first trophy under the new regime, but on that occasion so were Liverpool. A Champions League encounter would be different. It would be about Chelsea justifying that massive expenditure. For once, for the Liverpool players it would be about enjoying the occasion, and seeing how far the ride takes them.

An interesting sideshow has been the fact that Liverpool could win the Champions League and, if the club finishes fifth in the league, fail to qualify as holders. Unbelievable, but true.

It would require FA intervention to request Liverpool's inclusion over Everton. It would be a brave (or criminally insane) organization that omitted a team who were Champions of Europe (and therefore, in winning a fifth title, entering a very select group of the continent's elite) in order to include Everton, who will have achieved nothing remotely 'Champion'-like.

But of course, such dreams remain highly improbable — and there is still more likelihood of pipping our stuttering neighbours once the pressure starts to heat up, and once we've played our game in hand — Blackburn at Anfield

— and the home leg of this season's Merseyside derby. Once those two home games are played, there will still be as many home games left as those away (four of each). We've been in this position before and succeeded. They will start to feel the pressure as soon as they start to believe they have it in the bag, and it's theirs for the losing. Up until now they've had nothing to lose. But once they start dreaming of next season — and they will — they may well come unstuck, if they haven't already started to.

But I would gladly settle for fifth place if it meant an unforgettable night in Istanbul in May.

Why will Liverpool win the Champions League? *Why not. . . ?*

Discrediting Liverpool FC –
the world's best spin doctors
Summer 2005

We are the world's best when it comes to 'spin', aren't we? Politicians cannot hold a candle to us football fans. We can twist and turn any situation to our club's favour. Or, if we happen to be a fan of 'reverse spin' (no, nothing to do with shining only one side of your balls), turn any situation on its head.

We use spin on each other — as to why our favourites should play, and why those who madden us be taken around the back at Melwood and shot with an elephant tranquilliser dart — but mostly we use it on rival supporters: to defend our club, and rubbish theirs. As Liverpool fans we might be called into 'spin action' a lot more over the comical-looking Peter Crouch, should he arrive. But ultimately, does it matter a fig what fans of other clubs think?

People are still laughing at Crouch, fresh from scoring 16 league goals in 24 games. Personally, I'd like to see a bit more of that kind of 'ineptness' in front of goal at Liverpool. I'd settle for Laurel and Hardy, or Ike and Tina Turner, or Michelangelo and his dead clay-sculpting monkey as our centre forward pairings if they all notched at that kind of ratio. We all laughed at Andy Cole at Manchester United, but he scored the goals that won the league and was part of their Champions League-winning team. Was Cole the perfect player? Far from it. Did he do a job? No question.

I recently saw an Evertonian on a Liverpool forum, laughing that the Reds were looking to sign Peter Crouch. Such fun at our expense, less than a month after Steven Gerrard lifted the European Cup. You'd think the Reds had just been relegated to the Conference.

It seems no matter what your team achieves, there will always be someone who tries to lessen its significance in football's all-powerful whitewashing, white-lying, fast-spinning washing machine. But hey, none of us are perfect; we're all as bad as each other.

An example of opposition spin is the idea that Liverpool were 'lucky' to win the European Cup this May, despite the remarkable results against Olympiakos, and three of the big favourites: Chelsea, Juventus and AC Milan. It's very rare for a fan of a rival club to hold his or her hands up and say "fair dos, you won it fair and square. We bow to your all-round superiority". Frankly, more often than not we start lying to ourselves before we even begin lying to anyone else.

To be perfectly honest, I don't really care much for discussing football online with non-Liverpool fans. Unless they are incredibly well-balanced and open-minded, it ends up being the kind of argument I thought I'd left behind when I graduated from primary school. (And as my father was was an unusually growth-stunted circus dwarf descended from the Mbuti pygmy people of the Ituri Rainforest, I was always on sticky ground as to whose dad was biggest.)

Too little of it ends up being good natured and good humoured, and instead of clever badinage it just descends into rabid name calling. Banter is all well and good, but what you mostly find on internet fora, when it comes to inter-team discussions, is bile. Football has moved on. We no longer hurl broken seats at one and other; instead we launch catty epithets via our keyboard.

Your striker is a bit rubbish . . .

Oooo, Meeooww.

The summer of spin

The conclusion to last season provided one of the biggest opportunities for spin seen on Merseyside for 20 years. What happens when the bragging rights get a little blurred in their distinctions, and both parties feel they've won the moral victory? It becomes more confusing than the boxing world's hierarchy of titles, as to who is outright, undisputed champion.

Who is right? Does a fractional gap after 38 domestic games make you a better team, or does winning the European Cup? Again, I fully expect Evertonians to say the former. And that is their right — the life raft to which they must doggedly cling, to avoid facing up to the Reds' achievement in Istanbul. (Of course, ask them what they'd prefer: to finish three points behind the Reds and win the European Cup, or last season's scenario. If you get an honest answer, it would, I suspect, be the former.)

If you are playing the theoretical game of footballing Top Trumps, then nothing beats The European Cup. Only one of the achievements by Liverpool and Everton will be writ large in the historical archives of the game. Everton won the local skirmish; Liverpool won the World War. (Okay, the *European War*, but that sounds a bit crap.)

Again, I don't expect Evertonians to agree. But I am happy for them to think what they want, just as they shouldn't lose sleep over anything I have to say — after all, none of us is impartial, and nor would we wish to be. Ultimately, we don't have to justify anything about our club to any outsiders. And they don't have to justify their club to us.

Managing spin

When opposing fans say something, it's easy for me to ignore; but when their manager has a veiled dig at Liverpool's expense, I become interested.

I was rather intrigued by David Moyes' recent comments about everyone else looking up at a 'big three' of Chelsea, Arsenal and Manchester United. Now while I disagree with this on the grounds of what happened in Europe, in that I think Liverpool's major success there promotes them to form an elite band of *four*. I can't spin the Premiership table, in isolation, to make it look any rosier for Liverpool with regards to the points gap between 5th and 3rd.

I can offer the extenuating circumstances of injuries, but the Reds were too far behind the top three for anyone but Liverpool fans to take seriously the excuses behind the league failings. I'd like to think others would, but I wouldn't expect them to. But the silly part of what Moyes had to say was the following: how Everton now apparently compete in the transfer market with the likes of Middlesborough, Charlton and yes, you guessed it, Liverpool (the Champions of Europe).

Fair play to Moyes for milking last season's league table. If I were him, I would too. I fully expect Moyes to milk it until the teat is as purple as Alex Ferguson's nose (admittedly, that brings to mind some extremely disturbing imagery, if you picture it too literally). But Moyes was 'spinning' (something I've seen some Reds fans request he go do), because managers, just like fans, are experts in the art. Managers tell the fans of their club what they want to hear. And if he's our leader, we lap it up.

It was, however, a strange time for Moyes to make the comments, having only hours earlier lost out to Liverpool on the signing of the hugely promising Momo Sissoko, who had apparently also tempted Chelsea. It also coincided with Luis Figo pleading to join the Reds, who had also just signed 50+ cap Dutch star Bolo Zenden, Chilean boy-wonder Mark Gonzalez, and the in-demand Spanish international 'keeper, Pepe Reina, who turned down Manchester United.

Liverpool, it is clear, are competing with Europe's elite for players (it hasn't always been the case, in recent seasons), and not with the likes of Charlton and Everton. If a club in the list Moyes names makes a move for a player, and Liverpool do likewise, it becomes a mismatch. It happened with Boro's attempts to hang onto 'free agent' Zenden. There was no hesitation on his part. Liverpool still has that pulling power.

Everton had a great season last time out. By their recent standards. But to me — and here I'm employing my own brand of spin — it's like a Sinclair C5 (sprayed blue, Chang Beer written one the side) finishing ahead of a beautiful bright red Formula One Ferrari on the grounds that the Ferrari spent too long in the pits, because someone kept puncturing its tyres. (The tyres in this analogy being Cissé, Gerrard, Alonso and Kewell, not to mention several other reliable all-weather spares that were freakishly burst at various points of the season. Of course, it didn't help that some of the remaining spares were skinny and bald, albeit purely in a metaphorical sense.)

Of course, I have my tongue firmly in my cheek, and I exaggerate for comedic effect. After all, it's clear to all and sundry that Everton have rarely been good enough to compare even with a Sinclair C5.

(Note: this is not spin, but what is more commonly referred to as a 'cheap jibe'.)

Lying

Apparently, "the league table doesn't lie". But to my mind, the table is only "correct" once every team has played one and other home and away. But even then it doesn't take into account exceptional circumstances, such as unprecedented injury lists, and having Mike Riley referee your matches. All things being equal, the table wouldn't lie; but all things are never equal. It's part of the fun of football, but it's also a misleading element.

Look at it this way: Would Mike Tyson, in his prime, have been expected to box with a broken arm? Would he have been as fearful? — after all, he still had another perfectly good arm, right? But couldn't a mere slogger have stood a far better chance against him, with one of Tyson's arms in a sling? Given the choice, assuming running from the ring wasn't an option, I'd opt to face the incapacitated Tyson every time.

In football, if your best players are injured, there's no postponement to wait for them to be fit again, to make it a 'fair' fight. (Or, for that matter, facing a 'substitute' in the form of a lesser fighter.) That's part of the joy of football — the selection headaches of the manager — but also reason for occasional statistical anomalies.

At least that's my spin. But hey, what does it matter?

Ultimately, we'll go on celebrating winning Number Five, and Evertonians will rightly enjoy the summer they spent above Liverpool in the league table down to points won the previous season, and not, for once, solely on alphabetical order for the forthcoming season.

Reds will tease their Manchester rivals about the beautiful ratio 5:2, and United fans will mention their eight Premiership titles; to which Scousers will mention the all-time total of 18, and so on. Arsenal fans will counter Liverpudlian taunts about never having won 'the big one' with their remarkable Premiership record in recent seasons, and as for Chelsea — well, anything they achieve will be discredited by all and sundry on account of the "throw enough cash at a problem" factor. But will they care? I very much doubt it.

It's all about to start again. Ten months of new spin await . . .

Now That's What I Call Bravery
November 2005

There are different types of bravery in football. There is the hard-man who flies into a 30-70 tackle, with no regard to his personal safety. And there is the player who never hides, no matter how difficult things get, and who keeps plugging away.

The former are usually worshipped, for their obvious efforts for the cause. The latter aren't always as warmly appreciated. If by refusing to hide you simply make mistake after mistake, then you are just drawing attention to yourself.

Luis Garcia falls into this category: the way he keeps looking for the ball, and keeps trying to do that one special thing that can win the game. One of the problems Liverpool faced before the little Spaniard's arrival was that there weren't enough Reds capable of doing something different. It's skilful players who need this kind of bravery. While the easy pass may be the sensible option at times, there will be other occasions when only something unpredictable will result in an opening.

Harry Kewell will need to be brave upon his return to the side. I don't mean I expect to see him tackling like Graeme Souness, just that he has some sceptical fans to win over, and he has to stand up and be counted. One thing he might have on his side now, which was lacking in the past, is full fitness. If your fitness is lacking you can still find space and pop passes about, but you cannot burst past people with pace and strength. And when that's what you're expected to do, it becomes a vicious circle when failure leads to a denting of confidence. I always used to defend Jamie Redknapp against some of his fiercest critics, because he always made himself available for the ball, even when the Reds were getting taken apart or he himself was struggling. In Xabi Alonso, Rafa has brought us another such player, although one admittedly head-and-shoulders above Redknapp.

But one name currently stands out when it comes to having a tough time, and that's Peter Crouch. Anfield was very much behind him on Saturday, just as it always backs those who try hard. The most depressing aspect of Saturday's steamrollering of Portsmouth was the attention paid by the press to Crouch's misses, when he'd so clearly played an important role in the victory. It must be so easy to write match reports when supplied with such an angle, as it allows you to ignore everything else that has taken place. In some write-ups, the three goals Liverpool scored, and the three points won, were almost mentioned as an irrelevant footnote. *Oh, and by the way . . .*

It was very refreshing to read *The Times'* Oliver Kay say that there is some kind of media agenda against Crouch, even if not all journalists are participating. The main story on Saturday was not Crouch's failure to score, but that Liverpool won 3-0 and that Crouch had played well. Four convincing wins on the bounce, and I'm reading about 'failure'?

It takes a big man

Crouch showed his bravery on Saturday by taking the penalty, when he could so easily have stayed quiet on the edge of the area and watched Djibril Cissé spot the ball.

It was a nice touch that Cissé — from the usually selfish predators union — was keen to assist Crouch's search for a goal. Perhaps for that generous act, good karma saw Cissé's later wayward cross float in. While I believe Cissé, with a record of three from three, should have taken the penalty, I cannot be too harsh on a player who wanted to take responsibility. If Crouch had scored, it would have got the monkey off his back, and everyone could move on. While Crouch's all-round game and workrate has impressed me, the lack of chances falling his way in the early games this season had been a worry. He'd missed a couple of sitters, such as the late header at Birmingham, but in terms of a goal threat not enough was falling his way.

A lot of it has been down to the kind of service supplied, and just a general easing into the style of play. He has a good awareness of those around him, but given his unique playing style, it's taken time to integrate him, as can be the case with any new player. Saturday was the most dangerous Crouch has looked in front of goal. He may not have scored, but he forced several excellent saves, the most notable from his early bullet header. Other attempts lacked confidence, but he hit the target more often than not. And like Michael Owen when he was having a tough time, Crouch never hid. Late in the game, when the ball came his way, Crouch could easily have turned back and waited for support, but he kept trying to score.

Improvement

Results in the league have remained considerably better than the corresponding fixtures from last season. Isn't that what Crouch was bought to do, especially away from home?

Out of eleven league games played so far, only the Fulham result has been worse than last season. Of course, last season didn't leave a lot of room for things to get dramatically worse. But five games have seen a *better* result, including the two most recent wins, against Villa and Portsmouth, that were only draws last season. It's about turning draws into victories, and defeats into points. While I know it's not in itself an accurate marker, given all the variables, the logic remains strong: improve on last season's results on a match-by-match basis, and you will have an improved season. Improve results five times as often as you see a disappointing reversal, and the improvement will be marked.

One thing you can say for sure is that the Reds have caused more problems against the teams against whom they struggled last season. While the finishing hasn't always been to the standard expected, Rafa's men have been creating many more chances than last season. A good percentage of those chances are now being converted.

There are improvements in several areas of the pitch, most notably the back line, which is now looking resolute. It has taken just eleven Premiership games to top the amount of clean sheets in all 38 matches last time around. Again: indisputable improvement.

Clean sheets are the platform on which wins are built, but it has to be clean sheets kept without sacrificing attacking intent. Before Rafa arrived, the balance wasn't right. While things can always take a turn for the worse in football, the balance has been better this season, and excellent in recent weeks.

Several weeks ago I said that the European run last season only sparked into life once the defence clicked into gear, and that there was no reason why, once things settled down this season, the same thing could not happen in the league.

It's too early to say that the improvement is permanent, but that very thing is now happening. The Reds have been craving consistency more than anything, and a run of results that reads 2-0, 3-0, 2-0, 3-0 is precisely what everyone was looking for. What was most pleasing was that it continued after a two-week international break, with a heavily-rotated side as a result. The confidence has returned, a groove has been struck, and Liverpool are currently playing as well as anyone in the country, especially if you also take the Champions League games into account.

Peter Crouch has been an important part of the *team* that has been achieving this. It's not hard to see how much better he links play than Milan Baros, the more lauded but also more 'individual' player he effectively replaced.

Do we want a balanced team that functions beautifully and wins games, or the Real Madrid model of eleven disparate individuals?

Being ridiculed by others can make you stronger, more determined to succeed. Peter Crouch has experienced more ridicule than most throughout his career, and yet he has joined the European Champions and is likely to be heading to his first World Cup. Sometimes in life we have to be brave and not let our critics get to us; but they can also unwittingly inspire us to greater heights — no pun intended, in Peter's case.

Big Issues

Got Me Some Perspective
September 12th 2001

Liverpool Football club no longer needs a massive loss of life to put some perspective into the game of football. The two have been too closely linked for a decade and a half now. This is a match report, of course, but one looked at in a different light. On the journey north to Liverpool my friends and I listened in horror as events unfolded on *Radio Five*; and then, at a mate's parents' house in Chester, watched as the World Trade Centre collapsed live on TV. It was football we'd travelled to see, but the twin towers razed to the ground were not those of Wembley, those two landmark football towers earmarked for destruction this year. Alanis Morrisette, bless her cotton pigtails, seems to think she has ownership of irony. (Or what she believes to be irony; others might call it Sod's Law.)

So I'll remember the day longer than the match. This week I have been emailing people about the lack of atmosphere at Anfield, and mentioned the game against Wimbledon in March 1996, when a quiet crowd was brought to life by refereeing controversies; going for the title, the Reds had three goals disallowed in a 2-2 draw. So while I remember that match, it was another kind of black irony (very unlike rain on your wedding day, which is less ironic and more *fucking irritating*) that the match I spoke of was the only other one in living memory where I'd travelled to Anfield listening to a major news story unfold: the Dunblaine massacre, where a class of infants were cut down by some sick nutjob with a gun. I remember both the game and the events of the day, whereas in five years I won't remember much about Boavista, bar another picture book goal from Michael Owen.

A mate and I had also travelled to Anfield from London on the day of Princess Diana's death, only to get within half a mile of the ground before the realisation that the game was cancelled — deserted streets in and around Anfield; on the way up we regularly checked the radio for news, but it only seemed to be sombre chamber music, the kind that makes you want to crash your car. On that occasion matches were postponed on the day, with other matches allowed to be played the next day; this time it was the reverse — thankfully, as it would have been another wasted journey, but in retrospect, we might have been better playing Boavista at another time, when our confidence was higher.

So to the Portuguese: a lively, inventive side with quick pace and clever movement. But bollocks to that: what an absolute disgrace to the game of football. I've never seen a more pathetic collection of unpunished diving in my entire life. This was definitely a nadir. Any challenge saw them roll in agony, and one Liverpool challenge — on just one player — saw *two* Boavista men rolling in agony. At least decide who's going to pretend to hurt and stick with it.

On a day when tens of thousands, at initial estimates, died in New York, and thousands more were seriously wounded, with limbs torn from their bodies and skin flayed by fireballs, only to be finished off by cascading rubble, steel and glass, you had footballers constantly feigning injury, and then getting up and running around like teenagers. One guy lay on his side waving his arm hysterically for two minutes with more intensity than I've ever seen from in the most gut-wrenching war footage, but of course was back on this pitch after less than a minute of treatment. Maybe it's me, but I just found it distastefully ironic (only far more so than than the kind of 'irony' of a free ride when you've already paid).

Then, with the height or moronic stupidity and logic-defying insensitivity, the Boavista goalscorer (we'll call him Cheating Brazilian No.1) ran to the Kop in the third minute and proceeded to fire two imaginary pistols, one after the other, into the crowd. On a day when terrorism ravaged an English-speaking nation, you have a player with the intellectual capacity of flotsam and jetsam, pretending to shoot people. I'm just glad he didn't do the old John Fashanu 'plane' celebration.

It might be ironic — only in a different way to the good advice that the snivelling Alanis just didn't take, but Robbie Fowler gets a two game ban for pretending to take a recreational drug, in response to sick allegations he was a smackhead, as it apparently set an unacceptable standard for children, but it's okay for the kids of the world to see a footballer revelling in the delights of gunplay on a day of unprecedented mass terrorist slaughter? Someone should write to FIFA or UEFA about this guy, and this kind of celebration. If players want to keep pretending to shoot opposition fans, then one day an insane fan will actually shoot them back. Until then, it should be a mandatory red card. You get a yellow for taking your shirt off, and unless you are Jan Molby, where's the harm in that? Pretend to shoot 14,000 people and you're okay.

Maybe it's another irony (and thankfully I'm done with Alanis Morrisette quotes), but for a team of footballers happy to show us how tough they are, with their imaginary guns, it was amazing that the slightest contact had them acting like someone actually *had* shot them. They give it all the macho posturing, then act like snivelling wimps. Were it not such a sad day, I'd have been more saddened by the plight of the game, dragged down to the sewer by men not interested in contesting a football. Boavista had players booked for time wasting, four players were stetchered off, there was a spate of substitutions (each adding 30 seconds to injury time under new laws), and what — four minutes of injury time. It proved that with a weak ref, cheating pays.

What a dark day. Was it irony (of a very dark variety) that the last time we played in this competition 'proper' was on the day of great tragedy in Brussels? On the Reds' return it is to a competition unrecognisable, distorted by the new financial cash-cow where teams go to get rich before even thinking of winning the damn thing; on the day the world's most recognisable financial edifice is wiped from the sky. Somehow all the coincidences leave me uneasy. Because maybe it's not irony, just coincidence. Maybe I'm looking too hard for symmetry. Perhaps I'm not clever enough to tell the difference.

And what of our return? A mediocre performance, where we never got a full head of steam going. Steven Gerrard proved the centre is the only place for him, and was a class apart.

Still, it was better than Saturday. And Jerzy Dudek, who had no chance with three against Villa, was picking another unsavable shot out of the net after three minutes; we did, however, get to see two quality saves later on. He again looked bright and lively, and while Sander Westerveld would have saved both of those shots (unless in his Bolton mood), it's good to see the new boy settle in quickly. If legendary Dutch coach Leo Beenhakker says Dudek is the best keeper he's seen in 30 years, that's good enough for me. No one, not even Sander's agent, said that about the Dutch keeper. Whatever has gone on, it's hard on Westerveld to be training with the youth team — unless there are too many keepers to train for the first team (there are only so many nets), and he can at least get more time between the sticks to keep up fitness ahead of a decent move.

I don't think a point from the opening game is a disaster. (No, New York and Washington were disasters. A point about the semantics of these incidents: "It was like a disaster movie" say the witnesses of such atrocities. No. It was like a *disaster*. A disaster movie resembles a disaster, and not vice versa.)

You see? I can't even use words like disaster any more, words that all football fans use lightly. So I'll say that a point is okay, considering it was the first game of the tournament, and it's semi-acceptable to start nervously. It's all been hyped to the point where it's good to get the game out of the way, and we can concentrate on the group, and not just 'being back' in amongst the elite. A point is okay, especially as it was a point gained from being a goal down, not a point taken after having all three in the bag. We are a team better suited to counter attacking, even though it's not our only mode of play, so we should do well away from home. In two-legged ties last season we approached the away leg for a 0-0 draw to take teams back to Anfield all square, but these are one-off matches, and we can be more adventurous away, even if only on the break. And they will be played to packed houses, not to stadia like Anfield where only 30,000 people could be bothered to turn up. A landmark game in our history, in the biggest club competition on earth, not shown live on terrestrial tv, and people still aren't interested. Where's the need for a 70,000 seater now? It was a very poor turn out.

Football isn't more important than life or death, but it *is* important all the same: it's one of the main reasons we are happy to be alive, and surely that makes it relevant. Football matters. Life matters more, but football is part of life, not disconnected like some people would have us believe. Football *is* life, just as music and fine food and films and books and all the other things that go to make our time on earth something for ourselves and others to remember.

Football is life. And who would have thought it figured?

We never saw it coming

September 2006

So many things, good and bad, have visited themselves upon Liverpool Football Club in the last 20 years. And the vast majority of the highs and lows we simply never saw coming.

No one can predict the future (allegedly), but in the mid-'80s even the most prescient of psychics would have struggled to nail down what has since ensued at Anfield; and even had they correctly foretold events, they'd have been disbarred from UPAM (Union of Psychics and Mystics) on the grounds of unrealistic proclamations.

The preceding 20 years — the mid-'60s to the mid-'80s — were about the club, having already ascended the summit, pretty much successfully staying there; but from the mid-'80s onwards it has proved something of a frantic 'rollercoaster ride'. That phrase is indeed a horrible, tired old cliché, but it's hard to think of something that rises and falls so spectacularly (aside from Arjen Robben).

When trying to put into perspective the current status of Liverpool Football Club I always look back at the low points of the last 20 years, not just at the euphoria of the all-conquering teams. It's also important to remember how good (mostly) the last five years have been. Not perfect, but far better than the preceding decade.

Søren Aabye Kierkegaard (the 19th Century Danish existentialist philosopher, not the promising Brondby reserve left-back) spoke about living in the moment: how we don't appreciate life while it's taking place; that we only fully understand or acknowlege the true significance of events when we look back — sometimes doing so years later, when we're old, and regret the lateness of our epiphanies.

So before it gets too late in the day, let me take you back in time, like the Ghost of Christmas Past leading Scrooge back through his memories.

The year is 1990, the month is April, the venue Anfield. QPR are leading 1-0, before Ian Rush takes a difficult cross on his chest and fires home from an acute angle. Shortly after, John Barnes nervously converts a penalty via the post, and the Reds hold on for the win. Liverpool are crowned Champions for the 18th time, and for the 13th time in 26 years. Basically, for two and a half decades the following rang true: if it wasn't the Reds' year this year, it would almost certainly be next.

Who would have believed it would be the last taste of that particular kind of celebratory champagne? (Of course, the 1964 title was the first after a 17-year hiatus, and perhaps we're just the masters of coincidence and symmetry?)

The year is 2004, the month is June. The Reds have scraped into the Champions League by the epidermis on the skin of their teeth, and Michael Owen, the one man who guarantees goals, will take the chance to join Real Madrid. His expensive replacement will break his leg in an horrific accident soon after arriving, and Milan Baros, the only fit striker left on the books after Neil Mellor and Florent Sinama-Pongolle suffer serious knee injuries in January, will score just once in the Champions League after the opening group game.

In deep transition, the Reds will lose 14 league games. Given this information in the summer of 2004, not one person would have predicted the Reds would make it all the way to the Champions League final a year later. Frankly, it's ludicrous.

The year is 2005, and the date, of course, can only be 25th May. AC Milan lead Liverpool 3-0 at half-time, and the second half only kicks off once the referee has checked with television officials, double-checked his two Swiss watches, and asked the Italians to extinguish their cigars. One of the teams will score three goals in the second half. Admit it: it can *only* be AC Milan, right?

The year is 2005, the date January 1st. Southampton reserve Peter Crouch will join Liverpool in six months' time. It must be some kind of joke?

December the 1st, 2005. Crouch, without a single goal for Liverpool and England, and on a 24-hour drought, is the laughing stock of the media. There is no way in a million years that he will hit 26 goals in the next nine months — no way! — to take his total to 39 club and country goals since breaking back into the Southampton team a little over 18 months ago. Not only that, but it's an absolute impossibility that he would become the world's most prolific striker on the international stage for 2006, and the first England player ever to hit ten goals in a calendar year. I'm sorry, it just won't happen.

1997: Paul Ince is signed as the 'final piece of the jigsaw', to provide the steel to lift the title. 1994: Phil Babb arrives with the reputation of one of the finest centre-backs around, and is clearly just what we need. 2002: Bruno Cheyrou is the 'new Zidane', the goalscoring midfielder we've been lacking. 1992: Paul Stewart arrives after an excellent season as the holding midfielder at Spurs, and will be the new Ronnie Whelan. *Of course . . .*

2000, 1st October. Only three of the first eight league games have been won. Who would have believed the Reds would be the first club in English football history to fulfil every single fixture possible (when including European competitions), with not one single cup exit? Barcelona, Roma, Leeds, Arsenal and Chelsea will be beaten along the way to winning the League Cup, FA Cup and Uefa Cup.

2001, 13th October. Gérard Houllier, the man many fans have dubbed the 'new Shankly' following his remarkable Treble just months earlier, is taken ill at half-time in the game against Leeds, and narrowly escapes death thanks to smart medical attention. If no-one saw that coming, then equally surprising is how swift the Reds lose their way the following season, once 'Le Boss' returns to full-time management. (But not before coming within minutes of reaching the Champions League semi-finals.)

2002, autumn. Liverpool are given two eye-opening, jaw-dropping footballing lessons by an unfashionable Spanish team with an unknown manager. Rafael Benítez? Never heard of him . . .

1991, 20th April. Graeme Souness takes charge of his first game at Liverpool, in what can only be an inspired appointment. Who would possibly disagree? He has passion and knowledge; he captained the club with distinction, and was a quite outstanding player and fearsome competitor. He's also now a successful manager, after five great years in Scotland. But to quote Homer Simpson: *D'oh*! Rather than arrest the decline he will only precipitate it. After dozens of trophies in the previous 17 years, just two will arrive at Anfield in the remainder of the '90s, until finally the successful concept of appointing from within is abandoned. Which, of course, will never get the club anywhere.

1989, 26th May, Anfield. Michael Thomas, just two years before he himself will surprise everyone and become a Red, bursts through the Liverpool defence, in such a manner that Hansen, Nicol and co. literally don't seem to see him coming. A lucky ricochet and Thomas is through on goal. Time stands still. With hindsight, would Hansen or Nicol have opted to rugby tackle him before he lifts the ball over Grobbelaar? Or, in desperation, throw their studded boots at him? Only they will know. It is devastating, as the title heads to London with the very last kick of the season, but how much does it really matter?

Five minutes past three, April 15th, 1989. Like Highbury, or Highfield Road, the word Hillsborough means little more than any other stadium name, stirs no greater emotion. It is still just another venue for a big game — to all but those who are on the Leppings Lane terrace and clearly already know otherwise. One minute later, and the rest of the world will realise something is horribly, sickeningly wrong. Nothing will ever be quite the same again.

There's plenty we never saw coming. But very little of it will ever be forgotten.

Ninety-six spaces in the world

April 2006

Given the date, I've spent the last few days chewing over whether to address Rafa's rotation system, or the events at Hillsborough 17 years ago. It's easy to get caught up in the importance of the former — and football is hugely important to us all — but it's also easy to confuse it with the *real* importance of the latter.

Because we love it, and because it was loved by those who lost their lives, football goes on; it continued after Munich, and Ibrox, and Bradford, and Heysel, and Hillsborough; as well as the world's other football-related disasters: Kaizer Chiefs v Orlando Pirates, Spartak Moscow v Haarlem, Peru v Argentina. Football endures, but it never forgets. However, with the hundreds of fans crushed to death in stadia all over the world prior to 1989, in places as far-flung as Argentina, Russia and Nepal, it seems it took Hillsborough to finally learn some lessons.

In many ways I feel unqualified to speak of Hillsborough — I wasn't there, and at the time I didn't know anyone who was (although I now do). I wasn't directly affected by the tragedy, and yet, like all Liverpool fans all over the world, I felt it on a personal level.

April 1989 was an important, exciting time in my life. Just days before the tragedy I had turned 18, and passed my driving test. With the world opening up to me, I thought about all the things I could now do. With the FA Cup semi-final looming, I thought I could fulfil a long-held ambition and drive myself to my first game.

Of course, in my naivety it never occurred to me that the match would have long-since been sold out. But the intention was there. That it could have been my first game made it hit home a little more. I could have been one of those going to a game from which, little did anyone know at the time, the chances of not returning were 200-1.

I can still picture the route I drove as I listened to the match on the radio — or the first six minutes of the match, before chaos brought it to a swift conclusion. I was on my way home, and once there I made straight for the television, to watch in horror as the reality of what was taking place came flooding into the living room. I cried a lot that day, and in the weeks that followed. And that was just me, a Liverpool fan in another part of the country, detached from the real grief.

In 1994 I started playing for a football team that contained a Liverpool season ticket holder, Adie, and we became good friends, going to games together, home and away, regularly from that point onwards. He had been at Hillsborough (and Heysel), and yet had he been one of those who had perished in Sheffield, I'd never have known him; not only that, but his name would have meant no more to me than any of the 96 who lost their lives.

That's one of the strangest parts of life: the coincidental interactions and events that take place and that, had they not, we'd be none the wiser. There's a space in the world where once existed each of those 96 people; it's not just their nearest and dearest who have missed them since that day — although they are the ones aware of the fact. It is all the unmade friendships denied by cruel twists of fate, all the encounters that would have taken place; all the Reds that other Reds would have met at matches from that day onwards — except, because of events on the 15th April 1989, they weren't there.

Obviously you will not realise it, but some of you will have lost your future best friend that day, maybe even your future husband or wife. You lost future colleagues at work, or university, or in your football team or rock group. You lost the person who, otherwise, would be sitting next to you at Anfield.

Looking through the list of the 96 now, I'm shocked by the ages of the victims. So many were aged 15, 16, 17, 18 — at the same stage of life as I had been. All the things I've gone on to do with my life, good and bad, that I had no idea awaited me half my lifetime ago. Who knows what awaited those young boys and girls?

As a father, it breaks my heart to look through the list of those who died and see a boy like Jon-Paul Gilhooley, just ten years old at the time. Anything involving the death of a child reduces me to jelly. It is impossible to not empathise. Then there are those families lost more than one family member: the Harrisons, the Hewitts, the Howards, the Traynors, the Hicks.

Hillsborough hasn't 'ended'. Even now, all these years later, Anne Williams, who lost her son Kevin in the tragedy, is fighting legal battles, and setting up Hope for Hillsborough in the desire to achieve the justice she and others crave.

Despite writing regularly about the club, I've never claimed to be a 'super fan'. I support Liverpool for what the team means to me; not what anyone thinks it *should* mean to me, and not to copy what it means to anyone else. I've always been happy to admit that others are far more committed than I am, although I care deeply in my own way. I wasn't at Hillsborough, and only partly understand what it means to those who were; I will not pretend otherwise.

Having been at the game on April 15th 1989, my friend Adie is part of an unenviable group: the kind you wished didn't exist, for the sake of its members. So I always knew that, however dedicated I became, I could never be as deeply affected by all the issues surrounding the club as others.

But with a forum to express my views, it would be remiss of me to not take this chance to remind people of what was lost that day; and to think of the 96 people who exist in the hearts and minds of so many people, but were denied the chance to exist in the hearts and minds of so many more.

Anfield Is Dead. Long Live Anfield
May 2002

So, there we have it — a new stadium for 2005.

[*Erm . . .*]

The announcement was cleverly made at the start of the close season, so that it wouldn't distract from on-field activities, and so potential summer signings can be seduced by the new stadium's beauty — proof of a club moving forwards at pace. Or maybe they wanted the furore buried in World Cup fever — although I can't see too many Liverpool fans ignoring this topic because England are playing Sweden in a fortnight. Whatever happens, it remains a highly political issue — feelings run deep.

To me it now seems to come down to this: heart versus the head. All our hearts will no doubt say Anfield (as it currently stands, with a redeveloped Main Stand). But maybe now's the time to think with our heads. I fully accept Anfield 4 Ever's reluctant and dignified resignation on this issue. I hope that's an end to the matter. The last thing I want to see is a club split; some pulling one way, others pulling another, and the whole thing becoming a farce. That would sadden me beyond belief. The club could end up the laughing stock of world football. Do we really want that? Do we really want disharmony and disarray? Do we want postponements and procrastination and uncertainty, bickering and in-fighting? Pro-Move and Anti-Move protesters locking horns?

What worries me is that after statements from A4E and the Independent Supporters Association attested to a reluctant acceptance that progress needs to be made and that the ground move should go ahead, other (more radical?) opposing groups will spring up.

A4E were involved in discussions all along, after Rick Parry invited them in, and no one was more opposed to the original plans than they. But just as they came to give their blessing to the move, on the basis that it was the only realistic option, so, I believe, should all other fans; if it's good enough for those who cared so much and went to such lengths to make their point, then it's good enough for me.

There will be enough political opposition from bitter Evertonians looking to put a spanner in our works, and from local residents who can't see ("the wood for the trees"?) that the area of Anfield needs complete regeneration. The Friends of Stanley Park will also protest, even though Stanley Park's borders could be redrawn to include the land where once our heroes played. Surely kids will get a massive kick in knocking about on the very same patch of land that Liddel, Hunt, Dalglish and Rush covered?

Alan Edge, spokesman of A4E, said this: "We sincerely believed when we embarked on our campaign that an expanded Anfield would work given an exhaustive effort to make it work. Clearly, that effort has been made but has been found not to be adequate having regard to all the criteria required to be fulfiled." To me, that says it all. The club tried — it made the effort to look at every possibility. The best solution won. Just as you hold your hands up and say, like with Leverkusen away, that the best team on the night won, then you have to do the same here: the best solution won. You might not like it, but you have to accept it.

Change is one of the most important things in life. I think back to my 'best days', at two different offices where I used to work. I had great days at both. When I think back it's always with fond affection, and I sometimes wonder why I didn't stay at each place longer. And then I remember that most of the people I liked had moved on, and that I was bored with what I was doing after three or four years of the 'same old same old'. I moved because it was time for change.

Boredom is not a reason to move stadium. But memories are not a reason to stay in the same place. You don't stay with a spouse or partner simply because of the good old days — you stay because you have a future together. If you don't have a future, then you are wasting time living in the past.

Will Phil Neal no longer have won four European Cups if we move? Will our eighteen league titles vanish into the ether? Will the Boot Room, where Bob Paisley masterminded our greatest successes (making him the only manager in history to win three European Cups) be forgotten? Of course not. Time cannot be altered. But don't forget, the Boot Room was demolished almost a decade ago. The old Kop was destroyed eight years ago, and has clearly never been the same since. A lot of what we hold dear about Anfield is just in our imagination these days, alas.

The past is the past; in reality it no longer exists, but in our memories it is concrete. They can't take that away. Build a big monument after the rubble is cleared and replaced by parkland, saying "LFC Played Here". Tell people that it used to be the best stadium in the world, with the best atmosphere.

But in terms of an edifice in 2002, Anfield is clearly not the best stadium in the world; not even remotely close. And no stadium ever made a noise; just the people who inhabited it. And if the diehards neglect the new stadium, if they stay away in protest, then that is cutting off ten thousand noses to spite ten thousand faces. Liverpool FC needs the diehards to establish a new Kop. It needs fans to get behind the club and help make it the best in Europe once more. They need to care more about the future of LFC than its past. What do you care most about — our future or our past?

Mediocre clubs such as Derby, Leicester, Sunderland and Southampton have brand new stadiums. Arsenal and Leeds will be building theirs. So too will Everton, for God's sake. Some of these are/will be soulless, but anyone who's been to The Stadium of Light will tell you that the Mackems make some noise, and that the atmosphere isn't compromised.

While building to simply 'keep up with the Joneses' is not a reason in itself, it needs to be remembered that Anfield would within a few years become one of the oldest stadiums in the top-flight game; Newcastle and Manchester United have rebuilt more recently, and rebuilt more successfully, without the problems of landlocking that we are experiencing. I know for a fact from living in Leicester that the Foxes fans are sad to leave their home of the last 110 years, but they too are only moving a few hundred yards to somewhere a million times better. I'd hate to have seen Anfield slated by Bluenoses as a 'shitty ground' in a decade's time. It looks okay now, but it will date quickly. Built in a piecemeal fashion, it is not a beautiful stadium. It could be the rickety old Filbert Street of 2015.

I sat on the fence over the original plans last year. I wanted the club to progress into the 21st Century, but I didn't agree with a lot of what was proposed. I sat on the fence as I was confused; pulled this way and that.

A lot of the original problems have been eradicated in this revised plan. The capacity isn't over-stretching; we still struggle to get 45,000 to all games (although we can now sell 10,000 more season tickets), so a 70,000 seater could have been soulless for a midweek game versus Southampton. The name Anfield can remain, and the gates and memorials will be relocated (as if they wouldn't). We are moving a few hundred yards; if that's ditching our home, I don't see it fully — only to a degree. We are remaining in the Anfield area, not uprooting to the edge of town. The pubs will still be the 'locals'. Clubs need to evolve. Liverpool were one-and-the-same as Everton in the nineteenth century, before the split. The club once played with blue in its kit, before changing to red with white shorts, and then all red. If some of those monumental changes hadn't taken place we'd be supporting the same team as the Bluenoses. So change can be for the better . . .

If redeveloping the Main Stand at Anfield meant massive disruption for half a decade, then that's something to be avoided. We are back among the elite; we don't want to spend this time playing in a building site. If we want players of Djibril Cissé's phenomenal potential to join us, does Houllier show them a picture of a stadium with four different stands built at different times, or does he show them the images of the wonderful new stadium that will be ready in a couple of years? They will only care that it is 'Anfield'. And it still will be; it will be 'Anfield' — it will retain all that the legendary name stands for.

Football is at such a delicate stage in terms of finance. The future is not to be gambled with by overstretching — this was one of A4E's main arguments, and it is something they seemed to make the club think more seriously about. The down-sizing of ambition — almost halving the cost — is to be applauded. We don't want to be paying off the debts for the next 25 years. But we also don't want to keep having to rebuild Anfield every few years, or, worse, finally accept that we need a new stadium having spent fortunes on updating the Kop, updating the Anfield Road end, and so on; throwing good money at bad.

Parry recognised the need to keep the team strong; the First Division is littered with too many great stadia where the manager had no money to spend on the team; it is the great irony of modern football — build a stadium to attract the best players and then have no money with which to actually buy them. Fans will always flock to a nice stadium if the team is doing well; no one turns up to watch football at a bankrupt club after its doors are closed. In halving the cost, a 55,000 seater can still be an amazing sight to behold, and have a wonderful atmosphere.

The extra 11,000 seats, by my calculations (at an average of £500 per season ticket per 19 game season), should bring in an extra £5million each season in league revenue; another £3-£5m in cup revenue if successful runs are undertaken. Rebuilding Anfield to a 52,000 seater clearly wouldn't bring in as much. It would still cost lots to undertake, and the club would lose a lot of revenue in the process due to the reduced capacity during the works. Money is important in football, alas. How well you spend it, on and off the pitch, dictates how well you will do for years to come.

But the commercial side of LFC is now being managed very well — not to everyone's taste, not to my taste a lot of the time (I really don't need an LFC credit card application form coming in the same post as my season ticket renewal), but you have to say that Liverpool, unlike Manchester United, tries to retain a 'family club' feel. It doesn't always succeed, but the intentions are often good. It still cares about its fans to at least some degree, which is a novelty. The way Rick Parry invited in the Anfield 4 Ever campaign, to discuss its proposals, and kept A4E informed along the way, suggests that the club took the fans seriously. That it didn't simply listen to A4E and then ignore everything they suggested only enhances that view. It acted upon A4E's suggestions. A4E seem to respect that, and so do I.

A DJ on the Midlands radio station Century FM (I didn't catch his name, but he's a Forest fan) this morning said that he thought everyone secretly wanted to be a Liverpool fan. He was joking about the prospect of a mascot called Lily the Liverbird, and saying that it just wasn't Liverpool. His point was that LFC "stood for more"; LFC was different, had a greater integrity. And I agree.

But I don't see why having a new stadium — one fit for football for the next forty years — should mean dancing girls and furry prosthetics. Nowhere has the club said that it is going down this route — why should it sanction such tackiness? A club's image is about how it conducts itself, not the fact that the stadium itself is rich in history; after all, it was the players and managers, now retired and dead, who created that history. And it was the people on the Kop who made it legendary, not the bricks and mortar. It was the fans who sucked the ball in, not the stone terrace.

Our image is based around major success over the years. At its core is the wit and invention of Shankly. When thinking of Liverpool FC, people hopefully conjure a sense of the dignity of Paisley in victory, and of Fagan and Dalglish in the face of disaster and death. They see Houllier, overcoming illness. They see a large club that isn't perfect, a large club that makes mistakes like any other (McDonalds in the Kop?) But they see a club with has a different approach to the game, with (hopefully) a different set of morals. I don't see why the club is selling this down the river simply by moving into a wonderful new stadium.

I have seen so much knee-jerk reaction that I must simply question if people are stopping to think before reacting. If so, fine. But if not, think again. I'm just concerned that it is 'fashionable' to stand for the old values in the game — that's there's a pride in standing for things that unfortunately don't mean the same in 2002, alas. Of course football was a more honest game many years ago, built around the working classes. But football has changed, like it or loathe it. Liverpool didn't change football, nor did Italia 90 or Nick Hornby or Sky — it changed because of a myriad reasons, each an unstoppable force. You either swim with the tide, or you become an anachronism, a relic.

You don't have to sell your soul to the devil to move into the future. Progression should always have one eye on the lessons of the past. But if it has both eyes on the past, progression therefore cannot happen — you are simply looking back all the time, as you stand still. If the club deserted the Anfield area, that would have been ignoring the past; moving to Stanley Park isn't.

I want Liverpool FC to be a special football club for the rest of my life, not a museum or a shrine. Let's live the future. Remember our past, don't live in it, locked in your rooms at night with your videos of "LFC in Europe" instead of watching the match. The new plans just happen to include a museum and a shrine, and that's great; the new plans address the sensitivities surrounding leaving the present site. But the club itself shouldn't be the museum.

The architectural plans aren't perfect — my main concern is the open corners where the atmosphere can seep out. Surely it wouldn't cost much extra to fill those in and make it closer to 60,000? I understand that this is under consideration, and nothing is concrete yet. Yes, you need a designated home end, behind one goal, but it's the people who inhabit it that count most; apparently one end will be more capacious, so it's up to the people who sit there to make it something special in the manner of the old Kop. But on the whole I love the look of the new ground.

My main worry about LFC is that we move into the future, not live in the past. Too many of our failings of the '90s were due to living in the rose-tinted glow of the glory days; appointing Graeme Souness and Roy Evans because they were part of our 1970s/80s successes, when the way football was played and managed had changed. Finally Houllier has ended the old traditions, and brought about a new approach. What better time than to start a new chapter in our history than now, with such a bright future on the pitch to look forward to?

Yes, it will hurt. Yes, it will be sad. And yes, there will be tears from grown men who haven't cried in donkey's years. But it could also be a catalyst in finally reaching the pinnacle once more.

It's time to create some new legends, surely?

How I put football in perspective
21st September 2005

The Manchester United fixture is one I endure, rather than enjoy. There's too much at stake: losing hurts too much. Frankly, it's a fixture I hate, for a number of reasons: some footballing, some of a more personal nature. I'll never enjoy watching it, but I will no longer let it feel like the end of my world if we lose.

It may not feel like it at the time, but it's always just three points at stake. It's a fixture I struggled for some years to get into perspective, until I had no choice in the matter. Unless a comfortable lead is built up early on (and that's been a rarity since 1990, when Peter Beardsley completed his hat-trick after the Reds led 3-0 at half-time), it's only after the final whistle that pleasure, or relief, can occur. In fact, when the Reds are winning it can be even less enjoyable. Given a lead against United will invariably be slender, I always expect them to pinch their speciality late goal, and then you have the big plummet.

Five years ago United seemed unbeatable. They'd just won the Treble, and their superiority over the Reds in head-to-heads stretched back to 1996. (The 1996 FA Cup final was at that point the lowest I'd ever felt, in footballing terms, as a Liverpool fan. After the two league encounters I was certain we'd outplay them and win, but Roy Evans' players froze on the day. To this day I cannot buy a cream-coloured item of clothing.)

Then, on a winter's Sunday lunchtime at the start of the new millennium, Danny Murphy curled a free-kick past Fabien Barthez. Half-time quickly followed; and then every minute of the second half seemed to last an hour. A recent FA Cup game at Old Trafford kept coming to mind: Owen's early goal cancelled out by two injury time United goals. But this time the late goals never came. When the final whistle went, it felt like winning a trophy. Remember?

Since that day, Liverpool have won two League Cups (one against United), the FA Cup, the Uefa Cup, two European Super Cups, and a Charity Shield (also against United). In other words, won some actual trophies. Come to think of it, I'm also pretty sure we won something significant last season, but it escapes me at the moment. Any chance you can remind me, Sir Alex? United fell under the Houllier hoodoo, and for a couple of years every game ended with a Liverpool victory. That then reversed towards the end of his tenure, but beating United had stopped feeling like The Impossible Dream.

Much has been written about the parallels between football and life. While football is a religion to many, it's also easy to overlook that Bill Shankly was being ironic when he said it was more important than life or death.

In these last five years, I have experienced a series of highs and lows that, bizarrely, have tended to coincide precisely with the peaks and troughs of the Reds. Manchester United feature heavily.

I started writing for an independent LFC website in December 2000, shortly after that victory at Old Trafford. By the following May Liverpool had won the Treble. A season ticket holder, I only made it to the first final, against Birmingham; the 2nd and 3rd took place during my unfortunately-timed honeymoon in Spain. Life was good, as I savoured the remarkable events in Cardiff and Dortmund from a TV screen in a Spanish bar: ample consolation for not being at the games. The Reds won, and ultimately that was what mattered most.

The weekend in February 2002 when my son was born, the Reds, now so replete with confidence as to be challenging Arsenal for the title, won 6-0 at Ipswich. (It's a good job I never went through with my desire to name my son after the first Liverpool goalscorer that weekend. Little Abel Xavier Tomkins may never have forgiven me.)

But then it all went pear-shaped. Within a further six months the stresses and pressures of life had got the better of me. Liverpool's plight still concerned me, but my own life concerned me more. I had been diagnosed with M.E. (Myalgic Encephalomyelitis) a couple of years earlier, and the new arrival sapped the last of my energy. My wife and I separated, and I had to find somewhere new to live. Battling illness and depression, I was stuck in a rut of despair. The weekend I moved to rented accommodation — heartbroken at no longer being a '24/7' part of my son's life — saw the Reds face Manchester United at Anfield. I watched the game on TV, then moved the last of my stuff. The game could not more perfectly have summed up how I felt. Perhaps the football compounded my mood; it certainly mirrored it.

The moment Jamie Carragher headed back to Jerzy Dudek, and the ball rolled through the Pole's legs, leaving Diego Forlan — he who had not previously been able to locate the farm, let alone the barn and its door — to prod the ball into an empty net, it all seemed so apposite. To be honest, I never want to return to the person who got hysterical if the Reds lost, and had his whole week ruined by a bad result. If you put that much pressure on the team to appease your needs, then you tread a fine line. There is a danger for anyone who treats football as his or her Prozac. If you look to football to cheer you up, or to fill a hole in your life, you are skating on thin ice.

But ultimately, that's your call. Conversely, if your interest stretches only as far as to read the results in the Sunday papers, that is your business — not mine. We are all different, and how much a result hurts us or affects our life is something that we have to deal with in our own way.

Although my health remains pretty much the same (good some days, bad others), life itself is much better these days. Less than three years after that lowest ebb I witnessed, first hand, the heroics of Dudek and Carragher, as Liverpool replaced Manchester United as the most recent English Champions of Europe. Football still gives me the incredible heady highs, like the mind-boggling delirium I experienced in Istanbul, but I have learned to expect, and accept, the comedown. Life cannot always be rosy.

Football, like life, has a habit of coming back to bite you on the backside. Bad times eventually follow good — all teams, whoever they are, slump sooner or later.

But then, as a Liverpool fan, good times have tended to never be too far away.

The Greats

Ray of Sunshine

August 2004

Ray Kennedy, to my mind at least, is a mythical player. He represents what all significant players do to a young child discovering the game: the footballer as Superhero. They *are* football. It's as if there have never been players beforehand, and none will follow: in your mind, as a kid, they exist without historical context.

An early introduction for me to the glamorous world of professional football was as an eight-year-old collecting Panini stickers. There were two Kennedys on the Liverpool page, and they seemed special for that reason (things like that seem interesting to a young kid. Alan was not in Ray's class as a player, I'd later discover; but he still scored two winning goals in European Cup finals).

But there's another surname now synonymous with Ray, and that is *Parkinson*. It is the name of the disease with which he was diagnosed in 1984, and which has seen his health diminish over the following years. But first, I'm writing this about a footballer, not simply a man who is now very unwell.

I was asked to write a few words about Ray a couple of weeks back, and at first I declined — he is not someone I felt I was well-enough qualified to comment on, and subsequently do justice to. I was watching — but barely understanding — football at the time he took his talents from Liverpool to

Swansea in 1981. But I have come to realise that I may be capable of passing comment even if I wasn't fortunate enough to see him play in the flesh, relying on the television screen (and subsequently, in various Liverpool videos and DVDs). I may not be aware of everything Ray Kennedy did as a player, but I decided I could provide my subjective take on the man.

Born with a surname as famous as any from the twentieth century — arriving in Northumberland twelve years before his American namesake was assassinated in Dallas — he was a key component in writing Liverpool's own staggering headlines. The way he controlled the ball and struck home the crucial goal away to Bayern Munich in the 1981 European Cup semi-final — having been forced up front after Kenny Dalglish's early injury — highlighted the contradictions of the big man: good body strength in shaping to control the ball on his chest, before rifling a shot with his "weaker" right foot. High pressure, progress to the ultimate game in club football at stake, and he's cool, calm and collected. It was a colossus moving with the nimble skills of a ballerina. (Don't tell him I said that).

It was only in later years that I learned he'd led a 'double life': he'd not, as I somehow believed, been a Red since Day One; he'd been an Arsenal player, and a bruising centre forward at that. He was a key component of Arsenal's double-winning side of 1971, scoring 19 league goals that season — although it would have been nice if they'd fallen at the final hurdle in the FA Cup that year; but I'm not going to make myself bitter over a football match which took place when I was merely one-month old. When he arrived at Liverpool, centre-forward was the role in which Bill Shankly intended him to play. Things didn't exactly go as planned, and he failed to make a spot in the side his own, and found himself in the reserves.

The transformation under Bob Paisley from a big and burly centre forward to an artful left-sided midfielder in 1975 is still seen as the greatest-ever manager's long-term tactical masterstroke. To put it into modern context, it would have been the same as Gérard Houllier playing Emile Heskey at left midfield and miraculously ending up with Robert Pires. (Alas, that never transpired.) Of course, the main credit should go to Kennedy, as he was the man who took to the field and adapted so wonderfully. There was none of this tosh about being played out of position; good players are versatile. Each will have his best position, of course, but if you can control, pass, shoot, head — then you can do a job anywhere. From midfield, Kennedy managed to ghost in and score crucial goals, hitting ten, nine and eight in three successive league seasons from 1978 to 1980. But he wasn't a David Platt type, who offered little else other than goals. Kennedy was a *proper* player.

In later years, via plenty of video evidence, I got to see — and understand for myself — what people said about Kennedy: that he had an especially sweet left foot. That is the adjective people use: Sweet. It is used for other players too, although almost exclusively left-footed players, as if those who prefer to use that foot possess greater perception and vision.

He was a tall, upright kind of player — not compact and dynamic like Keegan, the real Superstar player of the mid-'70s (before 'KK' took to spectacularly falling off of bikes as a television "Superstar"). Watch Ray Kennedy run, and there seems no way he was a footballer; he was in the same club as Patrick Vieira and Chris Waddle in that he simply didn't look the part, didn't move naturally. Put a ball at Ray's feet, however, and suddenly it was the most natural sight in the world. It stayed close to his side like an obedient sheepdog. He was suddenly a master, in control, calling the shots. Some players are busy, but busy themselves in going nowhere; Ray took his time, but always got there, always arrived. In being upright, it meant he also played with his head up — the sign of a good player. You need time on the ball to be able to lift your head, and only good players get time on the ball. You also need to know your control is perfect to take your eyes from the ball and survey the field.

In many ways Kennedy's decline was swift. In his final years at Liverpool he knew something was physically wrong when he played, and found himself increasingly struggling to get into the pace of games. He'd had physical problems for many years, but his great fitness masked their seriousness and kept any real concerns at bay.

My main connection to Ray Kennedy — and what made me think I could write this piece — is that I can relate to this physical decline, having gone — in a matter of a couple of years — from being a semi-pro to being comprehensively tackled by a woman in a work's five-a-side. (Before any accusations of sexism are placed, I've played against female England internationals and been fairly impressed; this woman, however, was morbidly obese and, by the looks of it, had never kicked a ball before in her life. I tried to lie to myself and say it was merely down to her imposing upper-body strength and preponderate twin "blockers", but it was at that point I knew I was a beaten man.) It's a strange feeling, experiencing your body is failing you before its time, while not understanding why. Once we pass our teenage years, we are programmed to expect an inevitable decline; no longer invincible, we know we will weaken as the years pass. We just don't expect it to happen suddenly and rapidly, whilst in what is supposed to be our prime. Ray was in his early thirties and he probably felt about twice that age at times. Being beaten by far inferior players — so soon after being a European champion — must have shocked him; it must have felt like he was being tackled by a fat woman who had two left feet, neither of which was in any way 'sweet'. I have a different long-term illness to Ray, and I am not as unwell, but I can empathise with his plight.

I don't sense Ray Kennedy to be the self-pitying type, nor do I think that on balance he will look back and think he has had a bad life; in his playing days he got to experience things us mere mortals only ever dream of, and in a way had not one but two very distinct football careers. It is perhaps best to approach end of this piece with the amazing fact that here was a player who did the hallowed double (League title, FA Cup) in 1971 at one club in one particular role; he then topped that in 1977 with a more remarkable double: Champions of England, and Champions of Europe in the same season (and a fraction from the treble) playing in a totally different position. The "treble" he did attain was winning the European Cup three times.

So there's *Kennedy*. And there's *Parkinson*. But maybe it's his Christian name with which I should conclude : *Ray*. The rays of sunshine he provided to football fans everywhere; the rays of hope (and inspiration) he gives as an ambassador for his condition.

King Kenny, Still Throned
August 2007

My first game at Anfield. There he is, the main man: Kenny Dalglish. Unfortunately for me, he's only in the dugout, as manager.

It is October 1990, just a few months after King Kenny's last official outing for the Reds. In truth, he effectively retired himself as a player a couple of years before that date, but May 1st — against Derby, the same opposition as five months later — he finally hung up his boots for good following a 19-minute cameo.

It's one of my great regrets in life that I didn't see him play in the flesh. I got to see all my childhood idols, bar Dalglish and Alan Hansen, both of whom finally hung up their boots in the summer of 1990.

By that stage I had every Liverpool video tape I could get my hands on. It meant I could still marvel at the no.7's play. But it's a bit of a sad irony that only scraps of Dalglish's genius remain recorded for posterity, while every action of Luke Chadwick has been captured by the cameras.

The tapes I possessed showcased Kenny's sharp thinking, always a few seconds ahead of the rest. But he had the skill to match the speed of thought — no point thinking quickly only to miscontrol the ball or underweight the pass — and a real gritty edge to his play. For someone so gifted on the ball he was a tough cookie.

And for a creator of goals he was also hugely prolific: a 40-goal season in Scotland and a 30-goal season in his first year in England; and over 100 league goals both north and south of the border. In his first six seasons for the Reds he averaged 23 goals in all competitions. It was generally easier to hit those kind of targets back then, but even so, he was supremely consistent.

Of course, assists weren't monitored in those days; they'd have taken some counting in Dalglish's case, especially once Ian Rush was running onto his astute, inch-perfect, defence-splitting passes. Has there ever been a better partnership in English football? (Aside, of course, from Daniel Amokachi and Paul Rideout.)

What was more of a shock for me was when, a few years ago, ITV Digital began showing some old Liverpool European games from the '70s. I watched in horror as, in one game, Kenny shanked a shot wildly into the Kop. He was human after all.

While Dalglish was an undoubted genius on the pitch, off it he continues to impress me to this day. It's rare to hear him say a bad word against the Reds, or its manager of the day. When called upon as a TV pundit, he refuses to get drawn into stating what the interviewer wants. He knows that it's easy to blithely criticise if you haven't been there and done it. I can't recall him trotting out lame clichés.

Perhaps it seems at times like he says nothing, or states the obvious, or sits on the fence. But what he is really doing is acknowledging that a manager has to make his decisions for a reason, and that we are not privy to all the facts. (Although at times you sense he's being an awkward git, just for the hell of it...)

In stark contrast to Dalglish's laconic wit was his impressive handling of the Hillsborough disaster. He had such a dignity about him, and did the club proud in its darkest, most testing hour. But clearly the awful events took their toll, and within two years he'd retired, showing the signs of serious stress.

But it's as a player, in happier times, that he'll be remembered most. No other player in the history of the game, before or since, has ever looked so overcome with joy whenever scoring a goal. While modern players might spend time practising elaborate celebrations that say 'look at me, aren't I cool/clever/an Olympic gymnast', to a fan nothing is more pleasing than a player going crazy with glee and demented delight.

Some things in football should be beyond debate. I recently had to Google something relating to Manchester United (yes, I felt unclean, and was surprised it passed the safe-search filter), and stumbled across a piece on an independent United website.

I first laughed when the writer said Liverpool have never had an exciting winger to compare with Giggs, Best, Ronaldo and, er, Gordon Hill. Those fellas McManaman and Heighway weren't half bad, but of course, Kenny's greatest signing, John Barnes, was the most exciting — and devastating — talent of the late '80s. A double Football Writers Player of the Year and two-time league champion, he'll be remembered long after Hill.

But I had to laugh even harder when the writer (presumably from his padded cell) stated that Liverpool "have never had one player that could ever be described as a genius like Best or Cantona, or a Wayne Rooney." (If only from a literal point of view, that last comment is true: Liverpool have *never* had a player called Wayne Rooney.)

Given the writer could remember Gordon Hill from the late '70s, you'd have thought Kenny Dalglish's name may have sprung to mind. Y'know — the man who won six league titles and three European Cups as Liverpool's key player, while United could manage no more than the occasional FA Cup?

Even allowing for its obvious outrageous bias and tedious lack of irony, it backs up my theory that the saying 'football is a game about opinions' makes some people think their opinions are as valid as those who have earned the right to express theirs.

'I'm entitled to my opinion' may be the standard response, but frankly, I'd just as soon trust the insight of a monkey in the Amazon who's never seen a football match. After all, he's entitled to his opinion too. People with 'views' such as those from the United website should be visited by the Opinion Police, to have their keyboards confiscated and Opinion Licences revoked.

Some things in football should be beyond opinion. If ever there was a nailed-on fact, it's that Kenny Dalglish was a genius of a player, whose talent actually made a difference when achieving extraordinary success — the kind United still can't mirror, given it was both at home *and* in Europe simultaneously. Another truth is that, as yet, Wayne Rooney is nowhere near fit to lace Dalglish's boots.

Not only was he a genius of a player, but King Kenny went on to win league championships as a manager of two different clubs: with Liverpool, three times, and once with Blackburn. How many truly great players can boast such impressive management credentials? It's a select bunch.

But hey, I could waffle on for hours. Sometimes the simple statements get straight to the point where fancy words fall flat.

I think the Kop said it best when they said: [*clap-clap, clap-clap-clap, clap-clap-clap-clap*] *Dalglish!*

'Sir' Bob Paisley

February 2001

I was in Tenerife, almost five years ago to the day, when I heard the news. I was gobsmacked. It felt like my own grandfather had died. As the saying goes, I remembered where I was when I heard the news.

Bob Paisley had died.

Bob had been closer to mind than he had for a while, seeing as amongst my holiday reading was the newly-released hardback biography of Bill Shankly by Stephen F Kelly. So while I read about the most charismatic manager of all time, I was also reading about his indispensable sidekick, Bob Paisley, perhaps the brains behind the gusto. It was all the more weird reading about results played out on mudbaths on wet Wednesday evenings in the early sixties when lying in blazing Canary Island sunshine, and weirder still when I picked up a paper later one day that told of Bob's death.

I knew Bob had been suffering with Alzheimer's for some time, and it seemed especially cruel that someone who achieved so much should die of a disease that rots one's memories away. Not for him the chance of growing old and weak with the one compensation of being able to look back on a truly remarkable life. That remarkable life was wiped from its very owner's mind. A great man doesn't deserve that. No one deserves that.

I don't doubt that Bob was the greatest manager ever. When I hear all these current managers (such as Jim Jeffries and Walter Smith — i.e. *Scots*) say that Alex Ferguson is the best ever manager, it makes me so angry. Alex Ferguson has spent fortunes in his time, and has six Championships and one European Cup as his major honours in fifteen years in the English game. (Yes, for all the hype and the knighthood, that still reads as just one European Cup. And okay, Ferguson had success at Aberdeen, but he has been a manager over three times as long as Bob was.) Bob Paisley won six Championships and *three* European Cups in just nine years. The team Ferguson inherited was doing badly, granted, but please don't tell me they were anything other than a sleeping giant, with lots of cash and players like Robson, Strachan, McGrath and Whiteside — not quite in our class, but not total duffers either. It can't be said that they were anything other than underachieving.

I even rate Bob above Shanks — I really do. Shanks is the reason we are all here now, and that is set in stone. He rebuilt the club. But he did so with Bob Paisley at his side. So not only was Bob involved in our rebirth, he then took the Reds to that all important next stage — the stage where true greatness is achieved. And kept them there. The team Bob inherited had won the FA Cup in Shanks' swansong in 1974, but in truth it wasn't one of the best Liverpool sides. A lot of the players who had been the cornerstones of the 1960s side had retired or moved on — St John, Yeats, Hunt. New players were in their place, although the likes of Ray Kennedy, bought to play up front, and Larry Lloyd at centre half, were not looking as good as their predecessors. One of Bob's masterstrokes was turning Ray Kennedy, who looked like he had lost the fight for the job up front as a target man/battering ram, into a superb, skilful left-sided midfielder with a wonderful passing game. It's the equivalent of Peter Reid deciding to turn Niall Quinn into a tricky winger (and no, that ain't gonna happen). Bob took this team, changed it around, and bought new players. He made it his own. What Bob didn't have, and what gets him overlooked in terms of accolades, was a larger than life personality. Shanks was a master with words about the game, whereas even his own players had difficulty in understanding exactly what Bob had to say. A good player was "whassisname" or "wadjamacallit", and apparently everything was referred to either as the "gubbins" or the "doings". Though his words were muddled, the message always got through, and was crystal clear.

Then there were Bob's dealings in the transfer market which were, to be truthful, nothing short of remarkable. Faced with the crisis of the exit of Kevin Keegan — a Liverpool legend — he went out and signed Kenny Dalglish as his replacement: LFC's greatest ever player. Bob went on record as saying he would have wanted both Keegan *and* Dalglish, had he been presented with the option — but that would have just been plain unfair, and the other 21 clubs would have taken their ball away and sulked with "we don't want to play anymore".

I love Mark Lawrenson's story of when he met Bob Paisley to sign — he got into the car to find Bob sat there in his cardigan and slippers. In this age of 'flash' we would do well to remember that Bob was about the bare necessities. Look at the players he bought: Dalglish, Hansen, Lawrenson, Nicol, Souness, Whelan, Rush, McDermott — just awesome talent, and nearly all of them the Football Writers Player of the Year or a runner-up at some stage. I know the Reds didn't rely on fancy tactics back then, but if you buy players as good as that — players who could think for themselves — then half the battle is already won. These days it is impossible to have a monopoly on talent like that, as back then you were picking from the British Isles, whereas now the world is a manager's oyster. Liverpool now have the homegrown Steven Gerrard as our heartbeat, but Arsenal have bought Patrik Vieira, and he wouldn't have been an option for these shores fifteen or twenty years ago. Bob Paisley had a smaller area to pick from, and unproven talent from the lower leagues were his stock-in-trade. A lot of Ferguson's credit is for the talent of homegrown players, and yet the likes of Cantona, Yorke, Stam, Schmiechel, Barthez, etc, are the reason United are/were successful — without Cantona and Schmiechel they would have not made the essential leap to Champions. So whilst Fergie bought well at times, he too had a wider group of players to choose from. Fergie's buys weren't picked up from obscurity. Ferguson's buys were established internationals.

In 1981 you picked players from these shores, and you had to unearth diamonds in the British lower leagues or in Ireland or Scotland (Whelan, Nicol, Rush, Lawrenson) rather than always cherry picking ready-made players. Spurs had Osvaldo Ardiles and Ricky Villa, but the influx of foreign talent was a dripping tap as opposed to the Niagra Falls of 2001.

But ignore all this — ignore the great man's achievements. Forget he was the best manager ever. That's only half the story of Bob Paisley.

What I want to highlight first and foremost about Bob — what I want you all to remember — is that he was just a great man: an honest, fair man, who puts most current managers to shame. When I saw the awful loser and general moaner Alex Ferguson get knighted, and Bob, with his three European trophies, awarded nothing, it made me sick. So it's *Sir* Bob, from now on. This was a man who went to Rome in 1977 to help Liverpool lift the European Cup for the first time, going back to the place he helped liberate in a tank at the end of the Second World War. How many modern managers can claim such noble feats outside of the game?

Ferguson even suggested this season that Bayern Munich didn't deserve to win the trophy, and that United were disappointed, as they believe they are the better team. Bayern topped both of their groups in the early rounds: Manchester United neither of theirs. Bayern then beat Manchester United — not once, but both home and away. Bayern then beat Real Madrid home and away. So it seems that to defeat the previous two competition winners so convincingly as well as winning their group stages — and the final itself, of course — is not good enough. United, who have won the trophy as many times as Nottingham Forest, are of course the rightful heirs to the throne. How dare Bayern beat them to it? Would Bob have been so distastefully vulgar in defeat?

No great player or manager likes losing — it's what spurs them on, that avoidance of the sickening sinking feeling of collapse. But there's this quality a true champion needs: humility. He needs to know when the better team won.

You have to remind people of Sir Bob, as people want to forget — after all, since the advent of the Premiership it seems that achievements in the game no longer exist if they pre-date 1992. (I read recently about how Andy Cole was one of the top scorers in the Premiership history, having reached 100 Premiership goals, and I thought how irked current players like Tony Cottee must be when overlooked, having scored bags of league goals when it was the plain old First Division. And I keep reading how the Reds have never won the Premiership, as if the Premiership is anything other than the First Division with a flashy new name. Eighteen league titles: I don't care what you want to call them other than that. Eighteen titles, six due to Sir Bob directly, and a good few more before and after his reign indirectly, such as when he helped out Shanks, as well as providing advice and assistance for Kenny Dalglish in the double winning season of 1985/6.)

In the end Bob himself forgot all he had achieved, and it is not right that the rest of football does the same. So please excuse me if I remind you all again in a few month's time — not because *you* will have forgotten, but in order that you may remind a few others, who support other teams, from whose minds he might have slipped. The Roma home tie is Bob Paisley Flag Day, and that's great, that's apt, but don't stop there: get carving that bronze statue now. I want to see it right next to Shanks, out by the front of the Kop, so the two great men of our history are side by side once more, and so they can scare the living daylights out of any opposing team who dare enter Anfield.

Ian Rush: Bow to the Master
November 2007

Apparently it takes one to know one. If it is true, then I, a far lowlier former representative of the Strikers' Union, should know a bit about what made the supreme master of the art special.

I've not seen many better finishers than the legendary no.9. I'd place Robbie Fowler just ahead of him due to a greater variety and panache to his goals, but in terms of all-round centre-forward play, and the sheer quantity of goals when at his pomp, I can't think of anyone better than the man from Flint.

In 1984 he scored 47 goals in all competitions. And this without being the club's penalty taker. It's beyond remarkable. This was when he was at his very best, in the years before he moved to Juventus in 1987; upon his return a year later there were fewer goals, but in compensation we also saw an improved footballer who, it just so happened, helped Fowler become the player he was.

I recall being at one largely unremarkable game against Crystal Palace at

Selhurst Park in 1993. It finished 1-1, and Rush scored. While he just managed one goal, that night under the floodlights he was phenomenal in every aspect of his play: workrate, linking, movement, and attempts at goal. Graeme Souness, manager at the time and, of course, team-mate of Rush's during the striker's first stint with the Reds, described it as the best centre-forward display he'd ever seen.

And yet it's now largely a lost memory, a forgotten performance. Even now I can't remember exact examples of what it was that Rush did so well, just the feeling of awe as I left the ground. Having started going to games in 1990, I'd seen him play in the flesh a number of times, but never as well as that.

Just over a decade before that Palace master-class, as a boy yet to reach to his teens, I was always over the park with my friends and a football. The obligatory jumpers down as goalposts and 'rush' goalie (no connection), we chased around night after night; playing until it was so dark we could no longer see the ball. And I was always Ian Rush. I even drank milk because the advert said he did. I didn't want to end up playing for Accrington Stanley.

Fast forward 14 or 15 years to April 1996, and I was stood at a urinal at the Moat House hotel in Liverpool as my boyhood idol strode up to the porcelain bowl beside me. Only hours earlier I'd seen him exchange those now-legendary passes with John Barnes — not so much a one-two from the great old-timers, as a one-two-one-two-one-two- (polite pause while defenders unravel themselves) -one-two — before Stan Collymore blasted the winner in the first 4-3 against Newcastle.

At the urinal to the other side of Rush was an acquaintance of his, asking if he'd decided on his destination after Liverpool, who were releasing him. Rushie (whose aim thankfully remained true, even at 1am), said it would be Leeds, and I felt I had a scoop on the rest of the world. It was a surreal moment, but, I sensed, not really the appropriate time to ask for an autograph. (Or, in case nerves stopped me from getting the final word out, asking if he'd let me have the honour of shaking his hand.)

We learn by copying others. And imitation is the most sincere form of flattery. So in many ways, the greatest compliment I can personally pay the legendary no.9 is that throughout my life I modelled my game on his. (Well, that was the aim.)

I could talk milestone figures relating to his goals — like 346 and 229 — or describe a number of finishes that we've all seen a thousand times, but for me, from a personal perspective, my most sincere compliment is that I wanted to be the next Ian Rush. (Of course, I was lucky in that I grew up watching how it should be done, in a way a Manchester City or Newcastle fan my age no doubt grew up learning how to knock someone in Row Z unconscious.)

I could talk all day about Rush's myriad abilities in front of goal, but one aspect of the strikers' art stands out for me. He could finish in all kinds of situations, but it was in one-on-ones, usually fed by Kenny Dalglish, where he stood out. It's one thing having pace, but it's another to use it intelligently. And no-one made better runs than Ian Rush.

I may be wrong, but I imagine that a lot of people who've never played the game think one-on-ones with a keeper are the easiest chances. After all, it's just the striker versus the keeper. Simple, right?

But one-on-ones are like penalty shootouts to a centre-forward. Beating a keeper from the penalty spot is not the most difficult thing in the world, but of course it's the pressure that makes penalties so tough. The pressure makes technique go awry.

And with one-one-ones, just as with penalties, it's the thinking time that's the problem.

So much of a strikers' art is about instinctive, split-second reactions in a crowded situation, where there's no time to sense the pressure. So when you have time to think about what you're going to do — or more importantly, time to *change your mind over and over again* — it can lead to disaster.

They test composure, much of which is innate, but also confidence, which is transitory. If a player is low on confidence, and has missed his previous five spot-kicks, you wouldn't ask him to take another penalty. It would be insane. But a quick centre-forward cannot hide when he is played in on goal.

Of course, the good ones will still want those chances, as they know their luck will change. They have the right mentality. But even a struggling one can't pass the buck unless he wants to look like a total idiot. Once played in, you have to go for it — not start heading for the corner flag, or passing back towards your own goal.

I remember playing in an FA Cup qualifying round, and missing three on-one-ones. It's hard to explain what goes through your head in those moments, but the word 'clutter' springs to mind. There's a jumble of ideas and instructions, and you can feel your heartbeat increasing. When you're on song, you feel in control and more relaxed, but it's still never easy.

A ball falls in the box, and bam, you hit it. But when you pick it up just over the halfway line, you have to take several touches as, behind you, chasing defenders (who aren't slowed by trying to control the ball) scurry back.

You also have no idea what the keeper is going to do, so you need to size up his intentions while also keeping an eye on the ball. Usually, when Rushie was concerned, the keeper's role was actually deceptively simple. He'd set himself, stare down the approaching moustachioed maestro, then go and pick the ball out of the net.

Breaking the offside trap is always vital, and is where so many quick strikers fail, or where so many linesmen thwart them even when they get it right. But Rushie pioneered a type of run where he darted widthways in front of the defenders, so that he was already moving when the pass came. All he had to do was turn 90° and he caught his markers flatfooted.

And that was crucial. I think that so many quick strikers, who can afford to hold their runs a bit more to avoid the flag, want to leave the defenders completely in their wake. It frustrates fans, but I totally understand the impulse.

I know when I played I felt this way, because the moment you start approaching the keeper you naturally slow down to weigh up the situation. So you need a few yards on the last defender, who, if he gets close enough, will be slyly tugging your shirt and nibbling at your ankles. But Rush had perfected a way of getting in on goal with time to spare. No-one was going to catch him, even when he broke his stride. So many times he sized up the keeper, took it past him, and slotted home.

Years of watching Rushie when growing up clearly influenced how I later dealt with such one-on-ones myself: the willingness to be equally happy (and not conclusively deciding until the last minute) to take the ball to the left or the right of the keeper; if you telegraph your intentions, or have a clear preference as to which side you favour, a keeper will have the upper hand. And Rushie, naturally two-footed, was happy to take the ball either side.

Then there's getting the weight of touch just right so that the ball moves quickly and firmly past the keeper (so he can't get a hand to it), but not so far that it runs towards the byline; things I'd never been formally taught but which, looking back, must have filtered into my thinking from watching the master.

(Of course, for the record I must point out that, alas, most of my game did not resemble Rush's in any way, shape or form — it no doubt appeared to those watching that I'd modelled my style on Mickey Quinn when it came to workrate, Marco Boogers when it came to commitment, Carlton Palmer in terms of grace, and Martin Keown when it came to shooting straight.)

Of course, Rush could also slot an early side-footed shot past the keeper — something Michael Owen always favoured. The keeper narrows the angle, but if you're good enough you can sneak the ball through the available corridor.

Rushie's other popular method was to lift or dink the ball over the keeper as he sprawled at his feet. This type of finish is dying out, because keepers stay upright for longer; Pepe Reina is particularly good at this, following on from

Peter Schmeichel's lead. But in the days when keepers always went down early, there were none better at Rush than exploiting it.

Basically, Rush could finish a one-on-one in every possible way, and therefore was never predictable. So while there may have been more stylish finishers, like Henry and Fowler, or slightly more prolific ones, like Shearer (who also took loads and loads of penalties), there weren't many better in terms of all-round play, and certainly none who could hold a candle to Rush in a one-on-one.

For a number of reasons I only made it as a semi-pro, but were it not for Ian Rush and the lessons he indirectly taught me, I might have instead been the useless kid picked last at games at school. Without Rush, I could now find myself writing about needlecraft or, heaven forbid, something really stupid — like rugby.

So I really do owe him quite a lot.

Can Rafa rank amongst the greats?
Unpublished, 2006

Were Liverpool to win the Premiership title in the next year or two, would it be fair to say that it would put Rafa Benítez onto a similar level as Bill Shankly and Bob Paisley in the pantheon of 'modern day' Liverpool managers? Or would it still be too soon to judge?

How does Rafa rate so far? It's still very early days, and hopefully he'll continue in a similar vein for a number of years yet. But there's some way to go to match the best. And yet, after a wait approaching 20 years, a league title now would feeel like it was worth double, maybe even treble. It'd be like finding the actual holy grail.

Paisley won the trophies that matter most time and time again. His haul of six league crowns and three European Cups in just nine years — plus other trophies, like the League Cup and Uefa Cup — is unbeatable. Shankly, meanwhile, was the man who built it up in the first place, earning the Reds promotion in 1962 and the league title in 1964, 1966 and 1973, with Bob the loyal lieutenant by his side. He also won the Uefa Cup — the Reds' first European trophy — as well as two FA Cups.

Shanks never won the European Cup, and that's the one major blot on his record. Of course, Inter Milan's general manager, Italo Allodi, was believed to have bribed the referee in the 1965 semi-final, with the Reds 3-1 up from the first leg. It seems there was nothing Shanks' team could have done in the return leg to succeed, and lost 3-0 thanks to some incredibly dubious refereeing decisions. Shanks *should* have been the first man to take a British club the final, with a good chance of winning; instead, the Reds were beaten in galling circumstances. He would never get the chance to come close again, thanks to a failure to land the league title until 1973; back in the days when only the Champions played in the European Cup.

Expectations are higher these days, because of the phenomenal success between 1964 and 1990. Liverpool were a sleeping giant when Shankly arrived in 1959; his effect, with his vim and gusto, was comparable to a quadruple expresso. Shanks dragged the club up by its bootstraps, and took it to a whole new level. It wasn't that he simply matched the glories of the past, given the club had won league titles before, but that on top of this achievement he gave the club a special aura.

Kenny Dalglish is another whose reign is hard to judge, primarily because he was unable to have his side compete in Europe — the 1987/88 team looking as good as any on the continent at the time — while he also took over when the club was in extremely rude health. What Dalglish did that Fagan didn't was to rebuild the side, introducing a quartet of outstanding players who took the team to a new level. However, I also feel Dalglish left the club with inferior players to those he inherited in 1991; having said, it's fair to say that following Hillsborough Dalgish's state of mind was severely affected by those awful events and the repercussions. But for that tragedy his approach to the job would have been very different.

Rafa will, however, overtake Joe Fagan if he lands the league title. Fagan's achievements are perhaps the hardest of all Liverpool managers to judge. Two years in charge, two European Cup finals — the first won, along with the league title and the League Cup, to complete the club's finest-ever season. But he inherited such a brilliant side, with so many world-class players interacting with uncanny understanding. Fagan deserves the utmost praise for keeping it going, and helping the club remain on a steady course after the retirement of the irreplaceable Bob Paisley. But if Benítez were to match Fagan's haul — European Cup, domestic cup, English Champions — he will have done so when inheriting a team well off the pace domestically. Fagan, by contrast, inherited an awesome side, with not a Djimi Traoré or Salif Diao in sight. Anyone who does that will always have to accept that, unless they significantly rebuild that side, their achievements will never escape the context of their arrival. Due to Heysel Fagan never stayed around long enough to do that, and it's a great shame that we can look back on just two years of his reign.

The weight of pasing years also makes it harder to judge the achievements. Comparing eras is deep in pitfalls. The major difference in all the comparisons is modern day Chelsea, with whom there is no previous benchmark. Shankly and Paisley challenged and beat clubs who spent more money, but never had to contend with a club who were in a totally different financial stratosphere.

The one interesting thing with Shankly, Paisley, Fagan and Dalglish is that they either went out as champions, or were champions the year before they retired. Dalglish lost his way towards the end of his reign, but the Reds won the league in his last full season. Shankly never lost the plot, but between 1966 and 1973 he won nothing. Like Houllier, Shankly managed to keep the Reds in the top five. His finishes between '66 and '73 were 5th, 3rd, 2nd, 5th, 5th and 3rd, and in those days such 'respectable' league positions didn't come with the recompense of Champions League football. Unlike Shankly, Houllier — despite it being the time when a 4th-place finish came with higher rewards — never got to hang around long enough to take the team back in the right direction. But then you never got the sense that the Frenchman was capable of doing so, and had never taken the Reds to the very summit of English football.

All managers can suffer a severe reversal to their fortunes if they spend long enough in the hot seat. Houllier's reputation took an awful hammering in his last two seasons. It now looks foolish for so many fans to have felt he was like Shankly reincarnated. He just didn't have that aura possessed by the fiery Scot, and when Houllier's methods reached the end of their shelf life, and he could offer nothing new, his time was truly at an end.

I still feel Houllier sits towards the middle of the list of 'modern day' Liverpool managers. Not as bad as many make out, but not the total unqualified success we all expected after the Treble and the 80-point finish in the league a year later. It's clear that Houllier inherited a side lacking direction, and promptly gave it just that. He just couldn't sustain it, and halfway through his tenure that direction switched into reverse. As with Dalglish, the turning point seemed to be a massive trauma: in the Frenchman's case, it was the major heart problem that nearly took his life. Following that, like Dalglish after Hillsborough, his judgement seemed affected.

Rafa has already achieved something no other Liverpool manager has: namely winning a trophy in each of his first two seasons. But he needs a league title (or maybe another European Cup, if that's not too far fetched) to be mentioned in the same breath as the greats. When Shankly first won the league title, in 1964, it was some seventeen years after the Reds were last English champions. This season will be the 17th since the Reds' previously lifted the trophy. Hopefully the wait won't last much longer.

£11m — the Going Rate For a Genius?

October 2001

£11m! To our nearest rivals this season. £11m! Sell Robbie Fowler to Blackburn for £11m if you must (and please, *don't*), but to a team who could pip us to the title? Surely he must cost any decent 'rival' team £20m? If teams add a premium on sales to their rivals (and they do), then that means the club arguably valued Robbie at around £8m — little more than Leicester paid for Ade Akinbiyi. Of course, the best thing is to not sell Fowler at all. Then again, it's a bit too late for that, it seems.

Christ (or *'God'* . . .), I go out for a meal with my wife and some friends, and walk back through the door at 10.30pm, and within five minutes both my mobile and my home phone are ringing, and I have a Red in either ear, telling me Robbie is going to Leeds. Nah, I say, it's just speculation, but when I check Ceefax and see Ian Cotton's name, and the mention of a deal being agreed subject to a medical, I know Fowler's time is up. Come in, number nine . . .

I'm still not sure, as it passes midnight, that it's sunk in. I'm writing this as there's no point going to bed, as I'll just be composing it in my head as I try to make sense of it all, and I'll be awake till 5am if that happens. I feel very numb. Sure, no-one has died, but football is a funny game, as we all know. What *has* died is the pleasure of seeing Robbie score goals at Anfield in a red shirt. What has died is the future as I expected it. What has died is the Kop clap-clap-clapping "Fowler!" What has died is the hope of Robbie scoring 30 goals a season in a shirt emblazoned with Carlsberg.

I think this is a big mistake for the club — unless he wasn't prepared to look at a new contract, but I've not heard anything like that. I also think that for all Robbie's misdemeanours, he's been harshly treated. For me, he followed his hat-trick against Leicester with a man-of-the-match display in Oporto against Boavista, where he came closest to scoring, created a chance on a plate for Emile Heskey, and worked his socks off, only to be dropped (or 'rested') for the next three matches. When he came on in games after this, his rhythm had been lost, his confidence dented yet again. I've believed since then that it would be best for him (but not necessarily Liverpool) that he went elsewhere. To me, 'rotation' only seemed to apply to Fowler and Jari Litmanen. If you want four strikers, fine, but don't complain when they get disillusioned if they never get a fair crack of the whip. Michael Owen was above rotation on recent form but Emile Heskey wasn't.

If Fowler couldn't oust a man who hadn't scored for 20 games, what chance did he have when Heskey hit form? Heskey put in some excellent displays, but so did Fowler in those two matches before his three-game exile. Fowler also scored three goals. I'm not knocking Heskey, simply saying that to me Fowler deserved more of an opportunity than he got. Heskey always got encouragement from the staff; sometimes Fowler needed that, too, I felt. It felt like a criminal act seeing Robbie's confidence dented to such a degree by not being believed in in any way.

Suddenly we have just Owen, whose hamstrings are tight yet again, Litmanen and Heskey, the latter two being more creators than finishers. I'm not sure Baros is the answer. The kid is 20. He's not known as a natural goalscorer, and this season is the first time in Czech football that he's scored a few instead of just looked dangerous. He doesn't speak English. He's never played in a major league. Yes — he *could* be the answer. But if he were to play only a bit part, would he weigh in with 17 goals, of the importance of Fowler's last season? Given how well-positioned we are, is *could* good enough? Surely it's time to stick with the established players who know the way the team play? Why change things around now when it will only take an injury to Owen to leave us without a proven out-and-out goalscorer?

Part of me thinks that this has left such a big hole that I'm wondering if the club has someone big enough to fill it lined up. Is there a replacement, beyond the potential and future arrivals of Baros, Le Tallec and Simana-Pongolle? It's okay building for the future, but what about the present? It's so deflating to the majority of the crowd/supporters that it seems like the club is shooting itself in the foot. We were on such a high, and now I'm manning my phones like a samaritan after Take That split up.

If the club thinks Baros is the answer, then he simply needs to be at Melwood as soon as possible. But whoever comes in now will be forever known as the man who replaced Robbie Fowler. He will have to fill some big boots.

I've heard all the stuff about Robbie being overweight and not contributing, but last season he scored more goals than Heskey per start (17 goals in 27 starts), and scored in two semi-finals, two finals, one penalty shoot-out and two goals in the club's 'most important' game at the Valley. If that's not contributing, I don't know what is. He hasn't always behaved off the pitch, but Danny Murphy and Steven Gerrard have both been caught out drinking in the last twelve months, and they are both held up as model pros.

Sometimes it's better for players to go out and have a beer to relax than stay cooped up without any way to relieve the stress of playing; staying in just to get worked up about upcoming games. Both Liverpool and Nottingham Forest won cup finals in the 1970s after *insisting* their players got drunk the night before. Brian Clough wouldn't let his players leave the hotel bar the night before a League Cup final, which they won 3-1 having staggered up the stairs at 2am the morning of the match.

While times have changed, letting off the pressure without causing trouble is no great crime, as long as not done day in, day out.

I accept that Fowler is not the most deadly striker at the club any more — that's Owen. I've spoken about how our game doesn't suit Fowler any more, as it's all too quick and no-one (Smicer excepted) gets crosses in, but I was hoping we would tailor our game a bit, to find a way to counter attack quickly — but when that's going nowhere to utilise Litmanen and Fowler's more thoughtful link play. I guess that's a thing of the past. Perhaps the hope for a bit of subtlety in our play was hoping for too much; I guess it's back to defending 1-0 leads for our lives.

Why is this so hard to take? Could it be that nearly all of our real favourites have only been sold (or retired) when past their best? Dalglish, Hansen, Barnes, Rush — none left before the age of 35. Of course, Rush went to Juventus at the same age Robbie now is, but that was never going to return to haunt us in direct competition, and within 12 months he had come back anyway. Keegan, another legend, also went abroad, out of harm's way. But I fully expect Robbie to shine alongside Viduka, and I will be happy to see him score goals for Leeds (hat-tricks every week, albeit hopefully in 4-3 defeats).

I stay loyal to players I have idolised. I support Liverpool, but if you don't connect to the players it becomes a faceless, emotionless experience. Sean Dundee never gave me any joy and his departure was an irrelevance; Robbie gave me 171 wonderful drops of joy, and quite a few more other moments, such as the turn against Sunderland that left Williams on his backside, that led to the side-netting only, and the chip against Leeds (Leeds!) against the bar that led to them having two less points this season than they might have.

Robbie Fowler is a hero, the name and number on my now-redundant shirt. If I didn't go on wishing him well, then it will have meant that I felt nothing for him as a person or a player, and that he was just another humanoid clone passing through in the Red shirt. We only idolise players for what they have given us and what they can give us. We only idolise those who repay us most generously.

My desire to see Liverpool win the league has not diminished; however, my desire for Leeds to do well has just increased. If we can't win it, then instead of hell freezing over first, Leeds doing so is no longer such a bad proposition. Part of me wants to see Robbie Fowler prove the doubters wrong — part of me wants to see him put the ball into the inside of the side netting as only he can. I want Owen to outscore him, of course, but I want Fowler to score lots of goals. Not a single part of me wants to see him fail. As I said earlier, he can always score lots of goals in high-scoring defeats. That would keep me happiest.

So, to the future. I've got my ticket for Derby County. So having seen his first and last games, and first and last goals, I'll now see LFC post-Robert Bernard Fowler. It'll be odd. But that won't be as weird as seeing Robbie in the white of Leeds. Now that will take some getting used to. . . A Michael Owen hat-trick might ease the pain, though.

This article is interesting to me over half a decade on, as my opinions have changed somewhat in the last seven years. Not necessarily on Fowler, who remains a great finisher, but who has had a mixed time since leaving the club, and indeed since rejoining it. As I pointed out in Golden Past, Red Future, *Fowler's transfer fee was badly reinvested, and that remains the greatest crime here. The good news, of course, is that he returned for free and, presumably, on greatly reduced wages.*

However, in the piece in question I fell into the trap of having a favourite and backing him, irrespective of the results the team were getting; I based it on individual achievements and not the greater good of the team. While I thought Emile Heskey was going to be a sensation when he signed, I had grown tired of his failure to be positive in the box. But with hindsight Fowler and Owen were not the most natural pairing, especially with the way Houllier wanted his team to play. It might have been preferable to have Fowler or Litmanen linking play behind Owen, but that would have left Owen in a role that didn't really suit him; he could play on the shoulder of the last defender, which was when he was at his most dangerous, but could not hold onto the ball like a more physically imposing or technically gifted striker. Hence the need for someone big and strong alongside him. Unfortunately, Heskey's shortcomings tended to negate all of the positives he helped bring out of Owen. They were a good pairing, but not perfect.

While I see Peter Crouch as more effective than Heskey, I still felt happy to back the former during his goal drought, ahead of other players who might score more goals; the role Crouch played was what mattered most. Of course, Crouch has subsequently proven more prolific than Heskey, too.

Also, I was perhaps trying to excuse Fowler's misdemeanours. It's getting increasingly harder for players to unwind and relax, as the pressure on them grows with each passing year. Drinking out on the town can lead to aggro and news stories. Drinking at home, beyond the odd glass of wine, is not recommended in the modern athletic age. While there was no great harm in anything Fowler did, he also needed to change his attitude in line with the modern age.

Farewell Fowler, the Second *Going*

July 2007

At first I didn't believe it. Who did? Robbie Fowler return? A second coming for 'God'? Go on, pull the other one.

Anyone who surfs the internet will have heard dozens of such ludicrous stories over the years, as well as all sorts of even crazier left-field rumours. So many people claimed to have seen Thierry Henry at Melwood last month you had to wonder if the club was employing him as the new groundsman. And in years gone by Zinedine Zidane was spotted in almost every restaurant in the city. (Presumably even eating a burger with Elvis Presley.)

Except the Fowler one was true. He really was returning, as unlikely as it seemed.

For a while in 2005/06 it looked like Fowler really was rolling back the years. Five game-winning league goals followed once he broke his duck — fittingly against Fulham — in mid-March. His form propelled the Reds to their highest league points tally in two decades — 82 — although he could only watch in Cardiff as an ineligible player as another FA Cup was won.

While he couldn't replicate that form in his limited outings last season, his presence at the club was still a beneficial one. He was an important character in the squad, and his finishing in training remained an education to the other forwards, but Benítez openly wished Fowler had the pace and running power of Craig Bellamy, to create his own chances and finish them off.

I felt at the time, in January 2006, that snapping up 'God' was a great gamble to take, particularly as it cost only his wages. He was never going to be the player he was, but perhaps the magical mix of Fowler and Liverpool would give both player and team a boost.

In those first few months, Fowler justified Benítez's decision. While last season was different, and anti-climatic as far as Fowler was concerned, it could still have been so different had the other strikers been injured. He was little more than an insurance policy, but what insurance he provided; had he needed to have been called on, and thus had regular games to get into the swing of things, he wouldn't have let anyone down.

When I first got my season ticket in the mid-90s Fowler was at his pomp; the most natural finisher I'd ever seen. Without the legendary Ian Rush's pace, height or incredible stamina, he relied on finding the corner of the net from nothing more than a half-chance.

There's a difference between goalscorers and natural finishers. Quicker players and taller players will get chances by virtue of those physical attributes.

For someone like Fowler, at 5ft 9ins and only ever medium-paced even at his quickest, it had to be in his thinking and in his ability to strike a ball so cleanly.

For me, a natural finisher is someone who makes it look effortless; Alan Shearer, a great goalscorer, may have scored more goals, but so many were based on power, both in his running and in his shooting or heading. With Fowler, it was about timing, stroking a ball with inch-perfect precision.

A lot of being a natural finisher is about positioning, and reacting quickest, but that is true of most goalscorers. Perhaps what separates the two is improvisation: the ability to conjure a piece of magic.

A goalscorer with pace, when faced with a one-on-one with a keeper, knows he has to just drop his shoulder and he can go past him. Indeed, some don't even bother with such subtleties — knocking it ten yards and catching it up on the other side. A natural goalscorer will chip the keeper in an instinctive act, or curl it around him, and make it inch-perfect.

Whereas players like Rush and Shearer were obviously deadly finishers, Fowler just had that extra ability to do something out of the ordinary.

While his second spell at the club didn't highlight the prowess of his first eight years, the left-foot finish against Reading in the Carling Cup encapsulated his genius: it's hard to think of another player who'd have taken such a chance with the outside of his left foot and curled it into the *left-hand* corner as he faced the goal. Most would have used the inside of their left foot and gone for that side of the goal, or, if they did use the outside of their left foot, used it to curl it around the keeper in the more natural arc towards the opposite corner. But not Fowler. It was impossible for any keeper to read, let alone stop.

With someone like Shearer, you always knew what he'd do; he just hit the ball so hard few keepers could do anything about it. Why Fowler transcended Shearer during the mid-90s, in my eyes, was in the sheer artistry and unexpectedness of his finishes.

From a manager's point of view, a goal is a goal: yes, he wants to see good football, but if a goal wins a game, that's what matters most, not the aesthetics. But from a fan's point of view there's the issue of entertainment, of being thrilled. We all differ on how we balance out the need for points with the need to be entertained, but no fan could resist a showman like Fowler.

He was impish, and even appeared impudent at times, but his desire was always to score goals. He never wasted a good chance by trying to be too flash or clever; instead, he turned half-chances into sitters with his vision.

Fowler never lost that gift, but a combination of injuries and the massive speeding-up of the English game – and with it so many quicker defenders

– meant that a player who was not a natural athlete, nor a big bruiser, was always going to struggle.

Rafa Benítez is not an overly sentimental man. He proved this by omitting Fowler from the 18 in Athens. However, ten days earlier he had given Fowler 89 minutes on his Anfield farewell, only replace him, in an act of kindness, for a standing ovation. Typical of Fowler's luck in his second spell, it was just seconds before the Reds won a penalty, which he would otherwise have taken.

But while Benítez in some ways broke Fowler's heart twice over — first in Athens, then by releasing him — the boss had already repaired the biggest break of all by granting Fowler his wish to pull on the red shirt again, and have a chance to properly close the one chapter in his career that really meant something. And in that heart, broken or otherwise, he would have known this time, at 32, that his Liverpool career was finally over, and been able to accept the decision.

Also, in notching a further 12 goals for the club he edged past Kenny Dalglish in the Reds' all-time goals ranking, and that will be something he can look back on with great pride.

While Fowler's second coming will not be remembered with the fondness of his scintillating first, it gave both fans and player alike the chance to say their proper farewells. And that's something that cannot be measured by statistics or by trophies.

Sometimes being a fan is about something beyond your team winning and losing. It's about identifying with someone in the team, and appreciating the unique memories they provide.

In that sense, we all owe Robbie Fowler a big debt of gratitude. His heyday did not coincide with much silverware, but the memories are priceless.

Auf Wiedersehen 'Der Kaiser'
July 2006

It took me a while to warm to Didi Hamann. Perhaps like a lot of people, I was anticipating a different kind of player when he arrived in 1999, and my initial hopes and expectations were not met.

I'd seen glimpses of him for Newcastle, but mostly highlights including spectacular long-range goals. I was perhaps expecting a more attack-minded player; if memory serves, he was not an out-and-out defensive midfielder on Tyneside, but given more licence to get box-to-box. Seeing him in person when the Geordies came to Anfield in 1998/99 was no great indicator; he was sent off early in the match.

I may have been unfairly harsh on him during his early days at Liverpool, and failed to notice his silent, stealth-like ways. Or it could be that he took time to settle, and wasn't impressing in the manner he soon would. He arrived near the start of Gérard Houllier's rebuilding programme, and the team was hugely inconsistent. It took another year after Didi's arrival for the side to start really taking shape, and before long trophies started to follow.

I clearly remember my Road to Damascus regarding Didi; more accurately, it was a road to Rome. I made the trip to the Italian capital for the Uefa Cup game in February 2001, when two Michael Owen goals won the match. Hamann was utterly sublime, and my man-of-the-match by a mile. He was in total control. At that time, Liverpool had been out of the European elite for so long it seemed unthinkable that the Reds could go to the *Serie A* Champions-elect and not only win, but win with ease. We now take the re-found European expertise a little for granted, but the '90s had been a very humbling decade on the continent, especially away from Anfield. That victory was the turning point: a new decade, a new belief. Didi was at its core.

He was incredible in tight situations, always finding a route out for the ball, even if three opponents hemmed him in. He could keep the ball under such tight control, and then release it at the right moment. Of course, there was also his infamous routine to win a free-kick — amble in no apparent direction, then suddenly slow up and draw the foul as the opponent clattered into him. Priceless. You could see it coming a mile off.

Despite taking a year to fully warm to him I'm sad to see him go. But I do feel it was time for a change. I'd have loved to have seen Didi stay, as a member of the squad, but with the clock running down on his career the bench is no place to be. He's still too good for that, and will do well at Manchester City.

It's worth remembering Xabi Alonso was the 2nd-most successful tackler in the whole of the Premiership last season, and in the top three with successful passes, and to my mind he performs the deep-lying midfielder role perfectly, only with more creativity than his predecessor when in possession. The change in emphasis effectively signalled the end for Hamann at Liverpool. One limitation of the German was that he couldn't up the tempo of matches. Despite not being the quickest, if the pace of the game was fast, and opponents rushed in at him, he was brilliant; but stand off and instead mark the German's team-mates and he didn't quite have the creativity to pick out a colleague, nor the pace to charge upfield to get things going. That's not to say he wasn't a fine passer; he was. Just not in Alonso's class. The Spaniard can zip the ball at speed, and over distances, to get the Reds moving.

Alonso is also not the quickest, and as both men were most effective as the deepest midfielder, it made sense to supplement one or the other with a real athlete; while Didi and Xabi were capable of reading play and picking off attackers with astute tackles, someone like Momo Sissoko could chase and harry doing indefatigable 'doggies', to deal with situations where pace and stamina were required. Alonso was always going to be Benítez's preferred choice as the deep-lying playmaker, so Hamann became more of a squad man.

Despite a fairly prodigious haul of medals, Istanbul will remain his crowning glory. Having missed a penalty in Cardiff in the 2001 League Cup final shoot-out, he saved his Germanic spot-kick abilities for the Reds' two most important cup wins, the most significant of which helped turn Liverpool into the Champions of Europe in 2005.

However, I felt Hamann's contribution in Istanbul, while crucial, was a little overplayed by some. For me, it was the proactive step of going to a back three as much as anything else that swung the game; it helped that it was Didi being introduced into the middle, given his composure and experience, but any extra midfielder against Gattuso and Pirlo was going to prove beneficial if it meant freeing up Steven Gerrard and adding protection to the defence.

While taking nothing away from Hamann, the tactical change meant you couldn't judge his impact in isolation, in the way you could have had he been taking to the field in a straight swap. But he certainly deserves credit all the same. Central midfield is the strongest area of this Liverpool squad, and with the return to fitness of Bolo Zenden, there's one more player vying for a spot (even if Zenden would play further forward).

It's been a memorable and successful seven years, and Dietmar Hamann was as instrumental as anyone in taking Liverpool out of the dark days of the 1990s and into the new millennium, where silver became a joyously familiar colour once again. There's nothing left to say but "auf wiedersehen, Der Kaiser".

I'm not sure Didi Hamann ranks amongst the true greats at Anfield, but he is worthy of inclusion in this section on account of his sheer consistency over seven years at the club, and the role he played in several cup successes. For a while he was as good a defensive midfielder as could be found in world football, and his name is still synonymous with the role, as he enters the twilight of his career at Manchester City.

Shaken and stirred by the greats

October 2006

This week sees the culmination of a quite monumental countdown on Liverpool's official website: *100 Players Who Shook the Kop*, as definitive a list of Liverpool's best-ever players as you are likely to get.

The slight flaw with such a voting system is that the more modern players receive a slightly unfair advantage; while older fans are well aware of current players — I get emails from pensioners discussing Steven Gerrard — younger fans will not have seen many of the older players, and if they have, it is in limited television highlights from the days before every game was recorded. Meanwhile, players from the first few decades of the club's history stand little chance of appearing; we just can't judge them.

But on the whole I think it's an excellent representation of those players who have mattered most in the 114 years of the club. Some are recognised more for historic moments than consistent contributions; fellow columnist David Fairclough may not have got to start every game during his time at the club, but he made some telling contributions, and none more so than the decisive goal in the 1977 European Cup quarter-final against St Etienne: a goal that helped change the destiny of the club, as it moved towards becoming European Champions for the first time. Where would Liverpool FC be if, when faced with the French keeper, Fairclough had bottled the chance?

Michael Thomas, whose Liverpool career never really took off, helped win the 1992 FA Cup with a great goal, although he arguably shook the Kop harder than any opposition player, when, in 1989, he squirmed free with the aid of a fortuitous deflection to steal the league for Arsenal in the last minute of the last game of what was already the most emotional season in the club's history. Mark Walters' greatest moment was in 1991, against Auxerre; beyond that, and a 13-goal return in 1992/93, he wasn't the success people were hoping for. He almost certainly suffered from comparisons with John Barnes (who wouldn't?) Then there's the fact that sometimes we simply get attached to players who aren't necessarily up there with the greats. Mike Marsh was always a player I really liked, though he wouldn't be in a countdown like this. I just liked his style. Some people clearly felt the same way about Erik Meijer.

There are also the cases of unfulfilled potential. Liverpool rarely sold players before they had served their full use, but equally, few players were allowed to stay to the point of decline; Bob Paisley was a master at knowing just the right time to release someone. But a few of the players in this countdown saw their careers curtailed when they still had much to offer.

Mark Lawrenson was forced to retire at just 29, while Rob Jones had to hang up his boots at 27: both were quick and talented defenders. Both would have been higher placed had they not been cut down in their prime. Meanwhile an injury in 1991 robbed the Reds of the marauding wing-play of the mercurial John Barnes, but such was his talent on the ball and his quick-thinking that he found himself reinvented as a composed central midfielder. But it is his days on the left wing that will live longest in the memory, and which make him a bona fide legend. He had a balletic grace and a gymnast's balance, combined with a brutish strength that meant he could not be easily knocked off the ball. Matthew Le Tissier, no eight stone weakling himself, once commented that he went shoulder to shoulder with Barnes and ended up in the crowd.

There was also that change of gear in those early years that left defenders for dead, and for a winger he was also hugely prolific; so much so that he ended up scoring 28 goals as a striker in 1989/90. He was also great in the air; I lost count of the times commentators said "another rare John Barnes headed goal", having seemed to miss the fact that he scored so many that way. My favourite Liverpool goal, when taken out of the context of the occasion (so in other words, not Vladimir Smicer's in Istanbul, or other such crucial strikes) remains Barnes' second against QPR in 1987. Rangers were top of the league when they arrived at Anfield, but were sent back to London on the back of a 4-0 hiding. The goal in question came when 'Digger' won the ball on the halfway line and sprinted forward, drifting to his left past one defender before almost defying the laws of physics with a turn to his right which took him past England international Paul Parker. It would have been easy to blast a shot at goal, but he had the coolness and presence of mind to slip the ball under a young David Seaman, who premiered his look of bemusement mixed with dejection which he later reprised for Nayim, Ronaldinho, and Michael Owen at Cardiff.

I'm not sure a player's medals are an accurate way to judge his individual ability and impact. Clearly you need to have something about you to stay around for a long period at a club winning lots of silverware, but it doesn't mean you were a key man. Similarly, some great players never won the league title with Liverpool. Is it their fault that they weren't surrounded by better players, or the team given more direction from the sidelines?

I think the top 50, starting from Albert Stubbins, is where the list really starts to make sense, with token inclusions like cult-hero Erik Meijer filtered out, and where not one player seems out of place in this particular pantheon.

Gary McAllister is one of the few deservedly exalted stars who only spent a short time at Anfield. His experience was crucial in the 2001 Treble. John

Aldridge is another who came, succeeded, and left within a couple of seasons. Xabi Alonso and Luis Garcia have plenty of time to consolidate their positions, although they are obviously riding high on recent achievements. Alonso has been the more consistent of the two, and is one of the best passers ever to represent the club (and can only get better, at just 24), but perhaps no Red has scored more crucial goals than Garcia *en route* to winning the European Cup.

Jamie Carragher, at no.7 in the list, has come such a long way in the last two years. I was always a fan of Carra's, but I used to see him more as a vital 12th man, whose versatility was essential but who seemed a little limited wherever he played; now he's absolutely central to team. He really came of age at centre-back in 2004.

Six years ago I included Steven Gerrard alongside Graeme Souness in the heart of my all-time Liverpool team, which appeared in the club's official magazine. I'd already seen enough of the prodigiously-gifted 20-year-old to make such a bold assertion, and in recent years that faith has looked totally justified. My thinking was based on how good he would certainly be, as he had yet to prove too much at that stage. There's still more to come, as he enters the 'mature' phase of a player's career; allying his great physical attributes (pace, strength, stamina) to a greater level of experience. One thing's for sure: there's never been a more versatile player at the club.

That versatility may work against him in some ways, but it's a great thing for a manager to have at his disposal. I was fortunate enough to be present to see Gerrard excel in both full-back positions, going back to the early days of Gérard Houllier's reign: against Everton at Anfield, when he put in possibly the best right-back performance I've ever seen, and at Villa Park, when he moved to left-back after 15 minutes and looked like he'd been there all his life. Centre-back and goalkeeper are the only two positions in which I've yet to see him perform.

Robbie Fowler, like his mentor, Ian Rush, is that rarity in the list: the hero with two spells at the club. While Fowler's currently out of the picture (perhaps ahead of an important role in the second half of the season?), in his time on the pitch during this second spell he's scored some important goals at a very good rate. But it's his first period at the club, and the form he was in a decade ago, that made him a firm fans' favourite. It wasn't just the amount of goals he scored, but the way he did so. There was genius in the variety, imagination and subtlety in the way he found the back of the net. Not the quickest, and by far from the tallest, he could improvise and pull a rabbit out of the hat in any situation. If the shot was there to be hit by his less-favoured right foot, he'd use it. Rush, my boyhood idol, scored the most goals (although Roger Hunt netted more in the league), but Fowler was, to my mind, the more gifted finisher. However, Rush scored the goals that led to league titles and European Cups. Both were big-game players, but Rush regularly played in the biggest games possible.

So many great players. So many vivid memories. But who is the very best of the very best? For me, out of the two main candidates I'd narrow it down to it's still an easy decision.

The late, great Billy Liddell is an absolute legend; the team was dubbed Liddellpool, so that is indicative of the esteem in which he was held. But I only know of his genius from second-hand information, as he was clearly before my time. Sometimes you have to accept the received wisdom, and trust the older, knowledgeable fans. That he could still come in as high as 6th so many years after his pomp tells its own story. But Bob Paisley always said Kenny Dalglish was the greatest player ever to represent the club, and as he knew Liddell well, that's good enough for me. 'King Kenny' wasn't the tallest or the strongest (not that he could be bullied), nor did he have much pace to speak of. Clearly he was no athlete. But he had the ultimate footballing brain. There's nothing quite so thrilling in football as when a player sees something no other possibly could; sees something that we, as fans in the stands or watching on tv, with our bird's eye vantage points, don't even spot.

It will be interesting to see how the list looks in ten years' time. Hopefully it'll include a few current and future stars who help fill the ever-burgeoning Anfield trophy cabinet.

Steven Gerrard – Not World-Class?
July 2006, unpublished

Apparently Steven Gerrard is not world-class. It must be so, as it said as much in a broadsheet newspaper last week.

Yet more scorn poured on Liverpool's best players, on account of perceived failures when representing their country. First there was the laughable, baffling accusation of Jamie Carragher being a 'bottler', made by Sven's fitness trainer and turned into banner headlines by a certain newspaper. It's a complete contradiction in terms to accuse anyone who volunteers to take a penalty of lacking courage. Jamie Carragher stepped forward, and not for the first time in his career. Has anyone reading this seriously seen Carra bottle *anything*? I can only assume the Italian, talking about the player's heritage, meant he was a *Bootler* . . .

Next it was claimed that both Gerrard and Frank Lampard are not world-class. Does it really matter what people outside of Liverpool Football Club think about the Reds' captain? Arguably not. But it's still nice to see players receive their due recognition, and to not be 'as good as their last game' if that last game was disappointing.

Just because Gerrard was not at his very best in Germany (even though he was still one of England's three best players) does not change his status. He has played far better against distinctly superior teams on even bigger occasions. Man-for-man, and as a unit, AC Milan were light years ahead of teams like Trinidad and Tobago, Sweden and Portugal. And the Champions League final is a far bigger game than any at the World Cup with the exception of the final. I won't argue the case for the Lampard, as to my mind the Chelsea midfielder is a degree or two inferior to Gerrard, so that just confuses things; Gerrard can easily be world-class without the Chelsea man's presence in the same bracket. And frankly, I'm not concerned with defending Lampard.

Of course, much depends on your definition of 'world-class'. Is it the best handful of players in the world, or the best 50? Do you need to excel at international level, or does the Champions League count equally? Is being one of the best three players in one of the world's top (and most cosmopolitan) leagues enough? Or does being played out of position in a directionless side, and failing to be sublime, override everything that's gone before?

One thing I will say: if you asked all 32 national coaches at the World Cup if they'd want Gerrard in their starting XI, each would say yes without hesitation. France's, Brazil's, Italy's. And 31 one them would get more out of him than Sven Goran Eriksson. To my mind, that's the greatest failing of the departing England manager. It took Benítez only a short time to realise that Gerrard is a phenomenal attacking midfielder, either from a central position or on the right of midfield. Playing him in a defensive role gives you only half a player.

You could argue that the best players can free themselves of any tactical constraints and put their stamp on the game, but Gerrard was denied all freedom of movement and expression on too many occasions. Players cannot spend their time battling their own coach's shortcomings. And they can only take control of proceedings if given licence to; they cannot go directly against orders. Gerrard was not alone in Germany in being fettered when played out of position. All players should be prepared to play anywhere if asked, and do so without complaint. The interests of the team come first; but if the coach has got it wrong, you cannot then blame the player.

Thierry Henry, for all his consistent brilliance in the Premiership, has long had a tendency to go missing in big games. Is he world-class? Naturally. Henry did fairly well in the World Cup, coming to life for brief periods, but he wasn't his Arsenal self because it was a different system, and he wasn't supported by runners from midfield as he is under Arsene Wenger. The team play just wasn't there. Ronaldinho went missing in Germany, and didn't play a starring role in this year's Champions League final. Is he world-class? Of course. He's proved it often enough. Just as Ronaldinho was deployed in a role that didn't properly suit him, a task where the difficulty was compounded by what appeared to be confused tactics and a general malaise of the other players, then so did Gerrard similarly suffer.

While I'm not going to lose sleep over who captains England, if the national team wants to get the best out of Gerrard the new manager has to build his midfield around Gerrard, rather than have him simply fill the gaps as a kind of afterthought. He has to be the main man. The presence of David Beckham seems to overpower the rest of the players; five years ago he was capable of carrying the national side, now he's the most blatant passenger, but one whose 'image' dominates the entire squad. Gerrard had to defer to Beckham on leadership issues, and play second fiddle to Lampard on attacking duties. I don't fully understand that dynamic. Gerrard should be allowed to dictate the game, as the country's best midfielder, not simply be reactive. He should be setting the tone and setting the pace.

While Gerrard has some imperfections to his game, and room for improvement — like any top player — he is a wonderful all-rounder. And he is, to my mind, world-class by any definition. Look at his CV. He's just finished the season with 23 goals from midfield. He has now scored goals that have helped the Reds win the League Cup, the FA Cup, the Uefa Cup and the European Cup. That's not a bad collection of big goals in big games. He was also deservedly voted the Most Valuable Player in 2005's Champions League. That places him in a select club. Gerrard scored two goals in this World Cup, both from open play. He played in a deep midfield role in two of the four games, and sat out most of the remaining match. So that remains a top-notch striking rate for a midfielder, especially one inhibited by his role in the side. But that's now all water under the bridge.

The key thing from this point is that he shrugs off the disappointment, has the most relaxing holiday possible — physically and mentally — and prepares for a crucial season at Liverpool in which the momentum built over the past 24 months needs to be maintained.

I'll be more than happy to see him pick up where he left off in Cardiff.

In Praise of a World-Class Spaniard

January 2008

It's an end of the pitch where the difference is made, and an area where Benítez got it spot-on when mining La Liga. Get it right in this position, and you can win trophies and titles.

Yes, step forward Pepe Reina: to my mind quite possibly the best goalkeeper Liverpool have ever had. (And that lad Torres isn't bad either, at the other end of the pitch.)

I've heard Benítez say that praise can weaken you, and in many ways that is true; certainly when it comes to the first flush of success. But on the whole he doesn't buy weak characters who are prone to having their heads turned by a few kind words. And while Torres is winning the headlines, Reina, with a phenomenal 49 clean sheets in 87 Premiership matches, deserves all the plaudits that come his way.

If a striker had 49 goals from 87 games you'd call him world-class. But of course, a keeper can obviously only keep a maximum of one clean sheet per game, and in some matches will have no chance of stopping a goal. So to have a rate far better than one every two games is outstanding. (Then again, he could get a clean sheet without ever touching the ball.)

He'll be the first to admit that the defence, midfield and even attack play their part, but they'd also point out how much they can relax with him behind them.

For me, Pepe Reina mixes Grobbelaar's gymnastic agility with Clemence's concentration and composure. But he also — and this is a crucial distinction over any of his forebears — has a fair bit of Jan Molby's ability with the ball at his feet. His inch-perfect passing from the back, along with his super-quick thinking, is a big factor in turning defence into attack. It sets him apart from the rest.

While he's no midget, the only thing he lacks to make him truly invincible is the really imposing frame of a taller keeper such as David James.

Last season Reina made a couple of bad mistakes, as do all keepers, but Petr Cech has made as many gaffs in his last two games as did Reina all season. Over his two and a half seasons, the Spanish keeper has made precious few serious errors, and is on course for his third successive pair of Golden Gloves for the most clean sheets.

Let's also not forget the manager's role in organising the defence at set-pieces. Despite a couple of goals conceded from free-kicks recently (not helped by the absence of Hyypia as well as Agger to injury, and Crouch to suspension), for the first times in the league this season, the zonal marking system still has a remarkable record for the Reds. Chelsea have been leaking goals from bad man-marking, United conceded two in one game at West Ham, and Spurs have conceded five in their last two matches.

It's very difficult to foretell who will be a success, and to what degree. I've been wrong about players before, as I'm sure everyone has. I felt Cissé and Morientes could succeed; I still don't think either were 'failures', given that the former scored a decent amount of goals and played a part in the European and FA Cup successes, as well as the 82-point league haul, while Morientes played his part in the latter two of those three achievements. But Cissé never lived up to his price tag and potential, and Morientes never lived up to his reputation.

But with Fernando Torres I felt the most certain I've ever been of any player succeeding. Having said that, I still thought it would take him longer than it has to settle. So that's been a bonus. Other big signings, like Collymore, Clough and Diouf started brightly only to ultimately fail, but no-one has started their Liverpool career this well for years, spread over half a season. And it's no fluke.

I feared I might have gone too far over the summer in comparing him with Thierry Henry, and while they are different players (despite some similarities), Torres has the ability to merit the comparison. Now he has to show the Frenchman's consistency, season after season.

The Christmas period, and the Manchester City game in particular, has perhaps shown one of the toughest parts of adapting to life in England: lots of games in quick succession. Being a striker is all about lots of movement, whereas being a defender is often about taking a few steps here and there; reading the game, rather than running. So strikers feel it more.

Of all Torres' many qualities, my favourite aspect of his game is the way he takes the ball onto his left side, despite being right-footed. Sometimes he'll do it to get away a left-foot shot, other times he'll still use his right foot. When he does use his left, he can score goals: he has against Derby, Reading and Fulham.

One-footedness, and a proclivity to do anything possible to use the favoured foot, is a weakness in football. Some can get away with it: Patrik Berger was perhaps the best I've seen when it comes to a Liverpool player somehow working space to shoot on his favoured side, but if he'd used his right foot as well, he'd have been even better.

Torres' very first Liverpool goal, against Chelsea, summed up his unpredictability: the position of the ball clearly favoured a left-foot shot. But the problem was that doing so would take the ball closer to Cech, and any curl would possibly take it wide of the post; a right-foot shot could have the ball curl past the keeper and in towards the far post. Which is what he did. To perfection.

At the time I feared the finish (unlike the way he beat the defender) was less a clever decision and more a case of the Spaniard wanting it on his favoured foot. But the more I see of him, the more assured I am that it was sublime thinking, and that he'll always use the foot that the situation requires. For me, this is one of the most important things in a striker. It makes him impossible to suss out. While Torres' form may dip from time to time, he's as far from a one-dimensional forward as you can get.

How many times has he faced a defender and turned him square-on, only to breeze past him to the left? As well as the Chelsea goal, there was the run for the opening goal against Portsmouth, and the superb individual strike at Pride Park. The defenders know that they must stop him running onto his right foot, as he can do what he did in Marseilles: drift past players in the blink of an eye and finish with supreme accuracy. But that leaves them open to a left-side burst.

The willingness to use his left foot not only bamboozles defenders, but it also doesn't allow keepers to set themselves. His goal against Fulham came from an early left-foot shot. Against Derby at Anfield he also pulled a shot back across the keeper with his left foot.

Fifteen goals by the halfway point for a player who doesn't take penalties (unlike the others in the top-scorers' chart) is a great return, particularly as he's also missed quite a few games through injury.

I had a lot of correspondence about Torres over the summer, with fans expressing their doubts. But for me there was never any question he was the real deal. The comparisons with Morientes were as lame as you could get: both talented Spanish strikers called Fernando, but one infinitely more suited to English football.

Sometimes you have to pay a lot of money for top quality. But even at £20m, Fernando Torres looks a bargain. As does Pepe Reina, at just £6m. With these two young Spaniards, the Reds' should have years of success at both ends of the pitch.

Miscellaneous

Heaven Knows I'm Miserable Now

September 2005

I hadn't experienced so many miserable people since Morrissey and Marr disbanded The Smiths at the time of a worldwide antidepressant shortage. The location was LFC internet forums everywhere, the time this summer.

The higher the high, the harder the subsequent comedown, and innumerable Reds were still struggling to come to terms with a season that had mixed baffling underachievement with mind-boggling overachievement. Winning the Champions League did something really bizarre; it just made people unhappy. Or rather, it made them ecstatically happy and then, once the football resumed this season, it became a memory — a feeling that everyone wanted to recreate week after week.

Feelings like those evoked by Istanbul come along once every lifetime; even many of the veterans of Rome in 1977 said that 2005 surpassed the Reds' first European Cup, due to the unexpected progress to the final, and then the unimaginable turnaround after being 3-0 down. For a while, living in May seemed more appealing than living in August or September. Before Rafa arrived, winning the European Cup for a fifth time seemed as likely Gary Neville relocating to the Albert Dock and talking with a Scouse accent. It seemed the most elusive and unlikely thing ever.

But it happened (the European Cup bit, not Gary Neville), and in many ways everyone is still trying to come to terms with it. How do you top the highest of highs? Or, indeed, how can you simply follow it? In many ways, the success might have temporarily disrupted the progress of the Reds.

It's certainly made Liverpool more of a scalp domestically, at a time when the domestic form has come under close scrutiny, having been the area in need of most improvement. The opposition are lifting themselves that little bit more, almost as if they are playing the fully-fledged Liverpool sides of yore, who were used to such a reaction. Teams like Crystal Palace and Fulham felt they *were* the European Champions, because on one occasion they beat the European Champions. Every mistake the Reds make is accentuated by the critics' amusement at the 'fall from grace' of the European Champions.

The stability of both Liverpool Football Club and its fans — for the start of this season at least — might have been better served by redistributing some of last season's 30 wins in all competitions; so that instead of winning the Champions League, the Reds achieved a merely satisfactory outcome (losing narrowly in the last 16, for example), while winning a few more league games and finishing 3rd in the Premiership.

Despite some of the initial setbacks, and the possibility of it becoming a millstone, winning the Champions League can reap dividends in the long term, in a number of ways. Not only was it the kind of occasion every fan craves — those memories are priceless — but it proved to the players the heights they could scale, and taught them lessons they will draw upon for the rest of their lives.

It put Liverpool firmly back on the map, and also confirmed Rafa Benítez as the Spanish Midas. Not everything he touches turns to gold, but plenty seems to turn to silver. The top young players now arriving at the club — a good percentage of whom could be the stars of tomorrow — know as much.

The Champions League was the first major trophy (one of the 'big two') won by the players, and some may have been destabilised by the events. That it came during a period of transition — transition that would need to continue in spite of the success — only clouded the issue.

During the glory years, Liverpool's coaching staff insisted that players quickly retune for the season following a triumph, but that related mostly to players who had experienced giddy highs before. The first flush of success is the most potent, and it may have taken some of the current players time to find their focus. Just as failure needs to be recovered from, so does success. These players need to learn what it takes to be perennial winners, and not one-hit wonders. It was also a far less surprising form of success in the past, given it was achieved by firmly established Liverpool sides, and not ones in the very first year of a project.

The top-level success of 'modern' Liverpool began with winning the league in 1964 — which Shanks had been building towards for five years. Come forward a few years, and the first four European Cups were claimed when the Reds were by far the best team in England. There was more stability. The only comparable success was Joe Fagan's treble in 1984, at the end of his inaugural season, but he inherited the phenomenal side Bob Paisley bequeathed upon retirement.

It has been argued in the more recent past that the treble success came too early in Gérard Houllier's reign, but that was at the end of his third season, with a fine team which he had largely assembled himself. He just needed to have that side push on, having done half of the job, but after a promising spring in 2002, he appeared to lose focus in what it was he was building, and undid a lot of his previous good work, leaving a 'mixed bag' for his successor.

One thing a new manager can rarely call upon is stability, because of the necessary widespread changes. And without stability, consistency is harder to find. That's why it takes time to get things right. Just as you can't rebuild a house without first creating a mess and living through a fair amount of chaos, you can't seamlessly rebuild a side without experiencing difficulties along the way. Sometimes new players can create that mess; the uncertainty that arises from change, and a lack of understanding, both of teammates' play and the manager's preferences.

Nearly all new managers start with the foundations — the defence — and then work upwards from there. The attacking side of the game is always the most difficult to perfect, but it's impossible to have faultless attacking play if the defence is a shambles.

In the Reds' halcyon years, rather than rebuild, the Liverpool manager would merely add an 'extension' every season: one, maybe two players, to raise the level of what was already a superb team and to add a soupçon of freshness. Rafa's task was never so simple. But Benítez still had to take half of his house all the way back down to the foundations (carefully storing the infamous sofa and the table lamp for safekeeping), to rebuild it in a new style.

The work continues, but in the last three fixtures — two domestic, one in Europe — there has been a sense of what the manager wants his team to be about: stout defending, quick passing, variety and creativity when attacking, and comfortable margins of victory. Goals are at last flowing a little more freely. Perhaps the goals-for column would have been boosted had Luis Figo said 'yes' in the summer, but one thing the Liverpool board cannot promise a player during negotiations is Milanese weather.

With kidnap regrettably frowned upon by the authorities, Figo could not be added to the roster at Anfield, while Benfica changed the terms of the Simao deal at the last moment. So one area of the team was left temporarily unreconstructed. But even had a top-class right winger arrived, it would have been one more component to try and integrate, one further language in the dressing room. In some ways you want to make all your changes as quickly as possible, to allow them longer to settle and gel, but then you risk even greater disruption.

Now the squad is, at last, fully fit (touch wood), with players like Kewell and Morientes getting sharper, and the new boys are gradually settling in, we can get a clearer idea of where Rafa is taking the club. Any additions in January will hopefully arrive at a time when the team is settled and winning games, and can therefore be eased into the fray rather than called upon in desperation.

So it's important to look at what you have in football, rather than fret about what you have not. As with last season, if you balance out the exceptional European form with the more patchy domestic form, it still shows that Liverpool are a very good side. Not a perfect side — yet — but it proves there's something that can be built upon. Liverpool have to be doing a fair amount right in order for Chelsea to be envious of the Reds' European form.

Meanwhile, the amount of clean sheets suggests that, at the very least, the foundations are set firmer this time around. Improved defending in the Champions League proved the catalyst for glory in the second half of last season, and there's no reason the Reds can't go on a winning run in the Premiership using the same platform.

And on that base Rafa might just eventually construct our perfect dream house.

Exercising My Right to Remain Positive
23rd October 2005

Happy bunnies: they are an endangered species. And understandably so. There's not a lot to be happy about with regard to this season's domestic form. But while I'm not exactly smiling, I still don't see a lot to panic about, and as for those doubting Rafa: oh ye of little faith.

I choose to stay positive. Sure, I'm not expecting great things in the league this year, but I do believe that this team can gel in time for another Champions League qualification, and that's all I was expecting at the outset. (For a while we were desperate to qualify for that competition; now we've won it, and are doing well once again, but it's not enough.) Did we forget the work that was needed? And are we not going to give those changes time to come to fruition?

The teams currently doing well in the Premiership are mostly the kind of early pace setters who hit a wall by January. If it's true to say that a game isn't lost simply by going a goal down in the first ten minutes, then a season isn't over after a disappointing start. It makes things harder, of course; but nothing is decided.

I had been saying this season that if we continued to improve on last season's equivalent fixtures, then we'd end up with a lot more points. It's logical. However, I also said last week that if the Reds drop points at Fulham, then it leaves us back at square one, and that's where it feels like we've ended up. It is imperative that games like that at Craven Cottage are won. It's a kick in the teeth, but it's not a disaster. It's still early days. There are still 87 points to play for. Panic in sport gets you nowhere.

It was strange that Rafa went into this game with two up front — what lots of people have been crying out for — and the team was lacklustre and created little. When Cissé switched to the right wing, in a formation that was closer to 4-5-1, suddenly the chances arrived. But yet again, they weren't taken (partly down to Tony Warner's fine cameo).

I was happy at what looked an attacking line-up before the game. I have no problem with 4-4-2, just as I don't mind 4-5-1. Both of these formations have been used to win major trophies in recent years (unlike something like 3-5-2, with its wingbacks, which never led to any major trophies, and which top teams only revert to in desperation). But 4-5-1 gets all the unfair press.

The Premiership has changed from the days of blanket 4-4-2 in the mid-'90s. Manchester United fans chanting for 4-4-2 strikes me more a cry to be the best side again, and looking for any reason to explain their recent failure. To me, they no longer have the best players. Living in the past is not the answer. Do Blackpool fans chant for 2-3-5 formations?

So many teams play five in midfield (including Fulham) that it's an area where you need to win the battle in order to have any say in the match. When Liverpool play with five midfielders the chances have been arriving, just not being taken — by players who *can* score goals.

Form is transitory. If 'class' isn't seeping from every pore of the current side, I can at least see that there are some 'permanent' examples of quality at the club.

I wouldn't have been able to write anything in the last two years of Gérard Houllier's reign, as the football was directionless and torturous to watch, and positives were nearly impossible to find. The crucial difference was that Houllier was well into his tenure. He had built his team over the previous four seasons — got things precisely the way he wanted them — and as such, once the rot set in things were only likely to get worse, not better. He had a good stab at things, came fairly close to the league title, but ultimately fell short, despite the rewards of 2001.

There is a saying: guests are like fish — they start to smell on the third day. Managers are similar: they can start to lose their freshness after the third year. If a manager at a top club like Liverpool hasn't won one of the top two prizes in his first three years, his players may question his leadership. But good managers usually get better, year on year, in their first three seasons, and from then on even more so, if they've proved themselves.

Houllier never landed one of the 'big two' at Anfield, and it got ever harder to convince his players that he could. Unlike Benítez, I never felt Houllier could land one of the top prizes, for all the beneficial things he did for the club. Benítez took a mere ten months, just as he had with Valencia (winning the league). I don't see these as accidents, or in any way coincidental, especially as neither side was in perfect shape upon his arrival. Only the very best can work such wonders.

If anyone thinks Benítez won the Champions League in May with a great side, they are wrong. Liverpool were fully deserving of the title, as they earned it. But it was from a team playing out of its skin, and using all the manager's tactical tricks; a team that no one — no one! — would have believed capable of such achievements six months earlier. Again: any manager who can achieve such remarkable things has to be trusted and given time. If it means backwards steps along the way, so be it. Overhauling any squad leads to lots of new faces, and a lack of understanding. You might get lucky; otherwise it takes time to gel. Especially if you are taking over a team that was struggling, and lacking quality in depth (so unlike Wenger in 1996, and Mourinho in 2004).

Does it all feel like a backwards step at present? Sure. Are we struggling to score goals? Sure. Are key components still missing? Sure. But that's being addressed ahead of January, even if it has taken a few months longer than was ideal. If last season had been a disaster on all fronts, many would have shrugged their shoulders and blamed Houllier's legacy. The task would have remained the same this season: Rafa would have had 2004/05 to assess what he inherited, and begin building *his* team.

But by winning the Champions League, Benítez has made his own millstone. Where I look at it as proof that the man can work miracles, others now see only decline this season. The domestic form remains a worry. But it's not a problem Rafa cannot solve. English football is different to that on the continent; but not so different that it resembles another sport. Football men understand football; and what they don't at first understand, they learn.

But how much of it is to do with the difficulties of playing two fixtures every week, when most of our opponents only play one? This weekend, Manchester United and Chelsea could only draw games they were expected to win, and Arsenal limped to victory at Highbury. Last season, many of the teams in Europe saw their form radically affected by the extra midweek games; Boro were terrible until they went out of the Uefa Cup, at which point they finally found some form. This season, Boro are once again struggling, while Everton are having the mother of all nightmare starts to the season, and lost all four of their fixtures following their brief European campaign.

With so many teams playing five man midfields, they aim to stifle and overpower tired teams after their extra midweek exertions, and to make the most of extra time to prepare tactically. When Liverpool have had a full week to prepare for domestic games, the results have tended to be far better, if not exactly perfect. Does that tell you that Rafa doesn't understand English football, or that the players are struggling for freshness and that extra bit of spark? Perhaps rotating some of the players isn't helping, but then if you didn't you might have eleven tired pairs of legs, instead of seven. It's swings and roundabouts.

However fit footballers are, it's always easier if you haven't just played a game and travelled long distances in the previous 72 hours. That will always be the case, until we pay to watch androids. But it's a problem the other top teams face, and one that needs solving. So far this season, only Chelsea are dealing with it to the level that is expected, and they are the only club with the money to buy the kind of strength in depth that others can only dream about. (Bolton, meanwhile, continue to punch above their weight, but are behind where they were last season.)

In Liverpool's case, it's a mixture of problems: the poor form of certain individuals, mixed with a couple of key injuries and the rusty return from lay-offs of others, added to the handful of new players trying to settle in (and the players adapt to their strengths), plus the areas where strengthening never materialised, is all contributing to the domestic struggles of the team. *[An identical list of problems to October 2006, when the Reds found themselves in the same predicament, and again in 2007.]*

There are no *major*, unsolvable problems in any of these areas; but enough minor ones that are adding up to something more.

"Colossal"
March 2002

Quite, quite remarkable. Another amazing European night at Anfield. Roma must hate the sight of Liverpool. Eighteen years ago the Reds won the European Cup by defeating them in the final, made all the more humiliating by the fact that it was played at their own stadium. Then last season all the headlines in Italy ran: *We Want Revenge*. Except Liverpool won again, beating them 2-0 in Rome and progressing 2-1 on aggregate. So this must have felt like their chance for ultimate revenge, with the Italians having only to avoid a 2-0 defeat to go through.

Third time lucky . . .

Doh!

It's hard to place these latest events up there with our glorified past, and these days the superlatives are so over-used that the footballing public now accepts Sky's verdict that any 0-0 draw between Hartlepool and Halifax is an 'all-time classic'. This performance *cannot* rank up there alongside St Etienne, 25 years ago, when a victory by a two goal margin was essential once the French team pulled back an away goal. The story of that night is legendary. It is the one game where the team (and the watching crowd) realised it could beat anyone, go anywhere.

Not only was it an amazing night, it simply redefined the potential of a football club that had never won the European Cup before; within eight years, it had won four. The night David Fairclough slotted a bobbling ball past the French keeper is the stuff of legend; despite a capacity of around 50,000 at the time, if you believed everyone you spoke to there were closer 300,000 present, just as there were several million people crammed into the Cavern for the Beatles first gig.

But hold on a minute. You can't — despite Sky's efforts — immortalise a performance before the saliva on the ref's whistle has even dried. But I am almost certain that this will, in hindsight, be seen as the game where Liverpool Football Club came of age for a second time. This is the moment it made a mark in the 'big time' again; forget last season — or simply put that down to stage one: Bringing Home Some Silverware. This, with the team just two points off the top in the Premiership, was confirmation that following the success of last season the Reds have evolved into something altogether bigger. The return of a superpower? It's not unthinkable. But another reason that last night is already (in the cold light of day) something quite unique to remember (as the hairs on the back of the neck simultaneously stand on end), was the return of *our* superpower — Gérard Houllier. Looking gaunt (or healthy, if you conclude that the loss of unnecessary weight is a good thing), he strode out onto the thin gravel track running alongside the Main Stand hoardings, and took a massive hug from a friend: Fabio Capello (then again, any good coach in Europe is a friend of Houllier).

But the look on the Italian's face was betrayed by his clenched teeth, as if he knew there and then that Roma's task had just grown doubly hard. Houllier — already a legend on Merseyside — had stage-managed his return so that the players (who knew nothing of it beforehand) would be shocked and then, within a heartbeat, immensely motivated by his physical presence in the dressing room and on the touchline. The belief that only he can instill into the players' minds was there on tap, to be dispensed both before the game and at half-time, and even in the second half, from the technical area. And the crowd — already ready to whip itself into a frenzy and with Andy Knot again excelling on the Mosaic front — would take itself to a level of hysteria not seen (I'd imagine) since there were twice as many people allowed to congregate in that space behind the Kop goal.

Just as St Etienne is a legendary name to Liverpool fans, Roma is too. Perhaps it is *the* name in the history of our club. It was arguably the Reds' greatest achievement when, in 1984, the club won the Big Pot in front of a hugely partizan Roman crowd. The first win is always the greatest, but none can have been harder than that last one. Last year I was privileged enough to be in the Olympic Stadium to see Michael Owen's two goals that left us nervously defending a 2-0 lead at Anfield — the kind of lead known, disaffectionately, as the 'Arsenal 1989 Situation'. Avoid defeat by two goals and you 'win'. Liverpool avoided that 'defeat' thanks to the strangest piece of refereeing ever seen at Anfield (although it was never an intentional handball in the first place). Last night, Roma had only to sit on the 'Arsenal 1989 Situation' and they were through. They lost 2-0. They were out, along with Galatasaray, and after the ugly scenes of last week, justice seemed to have been done.

Perhaps Roma underestimated Liverpool at home, on the basis of the performance last season at Anfield, where they outplayed the Reds, who were caught between defending the two goal cushion and pushing for a third to kill the tie. Capello described Liverpool as 'one dimensional' before our group match in Italy. He must find it hard to sleep at night when his teams keep getting eliminated by the same one dimensional side; you'd think if the team were *that* simplistic, he'd have figured them out. It doesn't say much for his coaching, does it? That said, Roma had only lost two games this season, and none since before Houllier first fell ill. Roma are no mugs, no Finnish part-time fodder. These are the reigning Italian champions who just happened to be sitting at the top of *Serie A* once more. Real Madrid were the only team to beat them by two clear goals before last night. And Roma's success is built on their defence. It's just a shame ours was better, and in four games against the Reds in just over a calender year, they've scored a measly one goal. Liverpool have put four times as many past them. It says it all.

So what next for Liverpool? Where's the limit? If we continue in this vein (admittedly as underdogs both domestically and in Europe) and end the season how we ended last season, who's to say we can't repeat the famous double that we first managed in 1977. If we win all our games we are almost certainly league champions, and the small matter of beating the likes of Real Madrid, Deportivo, Manchester United and Bayern Munich doesn't look quite so bad when you realise that we've beaten Manchester United three times this season already, and outclassed Bayern in a 3-2 Supercup win.

Maybe the Queen's Silver Jubilee was a sign, a portent; this year, as she celebrates her Golden Jubilee, and the prospect of street parties returns to these shores, perhaps we can all use it as excuse to have our own party — our own summer-long street party, with or without the rest of the country. *[It turned out that the Royal Wedding of 1981 was a portent for 2005.]* The homecoming tour around Liverpool last season was one thing; this would be something above and beyond. But hey, I'm getting carried away.

The individual performances were nothing short of staggering. Henchoz and Hyypia are surely the best defensive pairing in world football. David Pleat was so overcome he described them as 'colossuses'.

Emile Heskey played like an absolute giant, and got a long-overdue headed goal, while Jari Litmanen finally got a chance to play behind two forwards. He excelled after some patchy displays — although it's hard to blame him as he has been used 'patchily'. Jamie Carragher seemed to have developed footballing abilities more closely associated with Roberto Carlos, i.e. wicked crosses at pace with the left foot and a turn of speed down the touchline to leave defenders in his wake. Such a surreal sight. John Arne Riise had his best all-round game for us, Danny Murphy played extremely well without catching the eye too often, and Steven Gerrard was just immense. The only player to have an (extremely rare) off-night was Jerzy, but he still kept another clean sheet.

But look at who Liverpool had missing: Markus Babbel, with illness, Michael Owen with injury, Didi Hamann, with a suspension, and Nicolas Anelka with ineligibility. Try telling me those four wouldn't be in your first choice line up? Plus Patrik Berger, who, although not at his best due to injury of late, would still be in mine.

I'd just love it — *love it* — if we drew Manchester United in the quarters or the semis. Five wins from our last five head-to-heads, but it gets even better: they are second favourites to win it, whilst we are rank outsiders. The pressure is on them: this is the trophy that we can almost call our own, but it's the one Fergie's obsessed with. They want it *so* badly. Whereas the pressure will be off us, as we have confounded the critics by simply making it this far; we are just happy to be in the draw, in our first attempt at this format. I, for one, never thought we'd qualify after one point from the first two games, but isn't it nice to support a club that continually astonishes you, as opposed to (circa 1991-2000) one that used to continually disappoint? *[Interestingly, the scenario I talk about here was what took place with Chelsea in 2005.]*

This season has to be the most topsy-turvy I can recall: a poor start; the keeper off-loaded and two replacements signed on the very same day; the manager almost dies; a brilliant run of results ensues; we then sell our icon to much disbelief; followed by some abject football; then we make a remarkable signing in Anelka; still poor football; then we're suddenly transformed into world beaters. Just like last year, we seem to have come good at the right time, as we used to in the glory days.

Phil Thompson may have played his part in our success, but it was one man's vision in overhauling the entire club that has got us to where we are: changing attitudes, diet, approach to a game; changing the personnel to the point where few of the players he inherited still exist at the club; changing tactics; changing training facilities, probably even changing the toilet rolls in the changing rooms and the tea bags in the tea trolley.

That man — Gérard Houllier — took a club living in the past and chose not to bring it into the present. He took it into the future.

Slightly embarrassing to read my own hyperbole about Gérard Houllier in the current context, but it had proven an emotional occasion. And at that point the club did appear on the verge of true greatness, and apparently far closer to being European Champions than at the same stage of 2005.

But we had no way of knowing that the last great masterstroke of the Frenchman's career at Anfield, when he returned to boost the team, had just been witnessed; it was pretty much downhill all the way from that point on.

As mentioned in the introduction to this book, I started to lose faith in Houllier midway through the following season, and 18 months before his departure, when it started to appear that he was not capable of finding a winning blend. All managers hit sticky patches, or have seasons when it just doesn't go their way, but the team was clearly regressing between 2002 and 2004 — and not regressing from an impregnable, dominant position, from which all the best teams have to sooner or later slip, but from merely a very good one, and thus headed down into mediocrity. Champions League qualification was missed in 2003/04, and only marginally secured at the end of 2004/05, while the only cup final reached was that of the relatively unimportant League Cup.

International Football vs Liverpool
October 2006 and November 2007

October 2006
I don't know if it's different for fans of other teams, but I know very few Liverpool fans who care more about their country's fortunes than that of the club they worship. The national team is secondary. For many, it's not even that important.

It's just a hunch, but I've always been under the impression that it is the fans of unsuccessful English clubs who care most passionately about the England side. When there's less chance of seeing a successful team week-in week-out, and there's no Champions League football for added glamour and excitement, it's probably more tempting to hitch your affections to the national side. England compete on the highest stage, and their fans always think they have a chance, however deluded that may be. For Liverpool fans, international football seems a mere hindrance these days.

It's been another fortnight of disruption for Benítez. No time to prepare for the visit of Blackburn last weekend, and three key players who would almost certainly have started returning to Anfield unfit for the game. Agger (the PFA Player of the Month), Sissoko and Kuyt have been three of the Reds' best players this season. Perhaps of equal importance, all three play in the spine of the team, which is clearly the key area to any side. Agger is a more progressive player than Sami Hyypia; the young Dane's passing and willingness to bring the ball out from the back makes him a valuable asset in home games, when more is expected from defenders in an attacking sense.

Some newspapers focused on the fact Blackburn had two Australian full-backs returning from the other side of the world, but at least they were fit to play. Those two do deserve credit, but they've not played anywhere near as much football this season as the Reds' key men. And the tiredness will catch up with Lucas Neill and Brett Emerton.

It's not like Liverpool don't have the depth in the squad to cope with injuries. But for all the talk of rotation, three enforced changes to the heart of the side meant Rafa's hand was somewhat forced. Injuries picked up on international duty are that bit more frustrating, as they are sustained fighting someone else's cause. (When they're friendlies, it's even worse.)

Benítez made the point before the Blackburn match that there's now a long period without these constant interruptions. But that run really starts now, as the weekend's game was still one of those that couldn't be fully prepared for. As a manager who thinks hard about tactics, the preparation time for games is arguably more crucial than to a manager who sends out the same eleven week after week with the instructions "more of the same, lads".

It's interesting that the same patchy start has plagued the Reds in 2005/06, and that last year it was only once the international games were over that the form improved. If there is a link, it's now up to the coaching staff to work out how to solve the problem. If it's a mere coincidence, then it's an unfortunate one. A title challenge isn't beyond the Reds, but it's only getting harder with every point dropped.

Let me be clear, though: I don't for one second think the Reds' average start to the league campaign has been solely down to the international fixtures. Nor is it solely down to rotation, if indeed it is down to that at all (given, like all conspiracy theories, it thrives on being impossible to prove either way; you can never *prove* results would have been better with different selections). Such simplistic arguments ignore a whole host of factors, such as poor finishing, myopic refereeing, integrating new players, injuries, uncharacteristic mistakes from defenders, tough away fixtures, and a lack of the kind of good fortune all successful teams need. It's a combination of complex factors. But the international fixtures have contributed, too.

I think clubs rightly feel very conflicted about international football. Complaining, however, smacks of sour grapes; it's the natural drawback of having the best players (although, of course, the problem also applies if you have a few Andorran and Lithuanian internationals).

Then there's the fact that if you deny players the chance to represent their country you're risking mutiny. Your players will resent it, and new players won't be eager to join a club if they can't play international football. Players see it as their divine right to play at that level, if selected.

It does have to be said that international football is good for the game in a number of ways, not least in how the World Cup introduces new fans to the game, and unites the planet behind one global event. It's the stage that all players gravitate towards, although the quality is no better than the business end of the Champions League, and arguably worse. Another bonus is the experience players pick up in international football, which clearly helps in their education.

There's also the fact that it presents a chance for players to play their way back into form without the result affecting Liverpool FC. Craig Bellamy is the perfect case in point: without that superb finish for Wales a week ago the ex-Blackburn man might not have placed such a confident header past the ex-Red, Brad Friedel. No goals in two months, then two in four days. Pepe Reina will also have benefited from a run-out for Spain, and his late block against Rovers was the young keeper back to his very best. Meanwhile, Peter Crouch's stature as a footballer has grown to become more comparable with his height following the most remarkable year representing England, and a record-breaking 11 goals in a calendar year.

The flip-side of this, of course, is that players can suffer a hard time with their country, as Crouch did a year ago, and have their confidence damaged as a result. The worry now, of course, is that Crouch hasn't scored in the last two internationals. How long before the backlash?

I also find it hugely frustrating that there's little accountability from the national teams towards the clubs. It is club fans who pay the wages of all international players; not those who attend international matches. And the clubs are not adequately compensated as a result of injuries. The international game as a whole cannot afford the insurance policies of top players, but some international federations do make a profit. Some kind of compromise needs to be sought. The English FA has one of the best insurance policies, but it still doesn't cover the full wages of its best players. I'm not calling for an end to international football, but the increasing professionalism of the club game, and the greater financial pressures involved, mean too much has changed in recent years to sustain the current model.

Another worry is that international managers don't have a duty to protect players from injury or strain; they are dealing in the here and now, the quick result to keep their job, and their next fixture might not be for a couple of months. That doesn't necessarily make them reckless, but once the international match is over, they are handing back a player whose condition is not really their concern. Arsene Wenger's recent analogy was excellent: "What the national coaches are doing is like taking the car from his [club manager's] garage without even asking his permission," Wenger said. "They'll then use his car for 10 days and abandon it in a field without any petrol left in the tank. We then have to recover it, but it is broken down. Then, a month later, they'll come to take your car again — and for good measure you're expected to be nice about it."

Wenger stopped just short of saying that the car then gets wrapped around a lamppost and torched. But that's what a serious injury to a key player must feel like to a club manager.

It's been a tough year for the Reds regarding international injuries. John Arne Riise missed the crucial Benfica tie following an injury for Norway, and Harry Kewell hasn't been seen since picking up a new injury at the World Cup. Dirk Kuyt missed just five games in five years in Dutch football, but he's already missed one for Liverpool after representing his country. And any chance of a transfer fee for Djibril Cissé this summer was wiped out by his terrible fracture when representing France; his future value could be affected as a result.

So it remains a complex issue, full of pros and cons — but for clubs who have shelled out fees for the players, and who pay their wages, there's arguably a greater percentage of the latter than the former.

November 2007

A couple of years ago, most England fans, judging by the way they treated him, would rather have had Peter Crouch in goal than up front.

Fast forward two years, and he is the only man this morning who can hold his head high (and no, that's not a pun on his size.)

I almost always want to see the England team do well (particularly when a few Reds are playing), but unlike when it comes to Liverpool, I am not a 'fan' in the sense that results affect me. I care … just not that much.

I look forward to the summer competitions with England participating, partly because it's the only football around at the time. Of course, like most genuine football fans, I soon get sick of the WAGs and the loutish fans, sick of the abusing of other teams' national anthems as well as of our own players.

But when the England national team and its wider issues start to affect Liverpool, my antennae spring into life.

As a result of last night's calamity, there will be calls to rid the Premiership of the foreigners who are 'doing so much to damage our game', and to have a quota system whereby a number of home-grown players have to feature in every game. Such calls were already being made even before England's depressing denouement.

These are the same foreigners who dragged English football out of the early-to-mid-'90s dark ages — a time when Andy Sinton, Carlton Palmer, Tony Dorigo, Paul Stewart, David White and Geoff Thomas were England players, and self-confessed alcoholics like Paul Merson and Tony Adams were regular internationals; a time when, before the 'foreign invasion', England failed to qualify for the World Cup, and European competition was too tricky for our nation's clubs. (In 1994, Barcelona absolutely humiliated Manchester United.)

These are the very same foreigners — including three continental managers — who helped the Premiership (and its best English players, let's not forget) find itself heavily represented in the last four Champions League semi-finals and the last three finals.

If there's one thing I hate above almost all others when it comes to Englishness, it's the blaming of foreigners for any malaise. You can find plenty wrong with any country and any culture, if that's what you choose to focus on. But the same applies to England, lest we ever dare look at ourselves through the thick fog of our patriotism.

Personally speaking, I'd much rather have a league that celebrates the best: the best players from around the world, allied to the best English talent.

I want to see talented English players, most preferably Scousers, in the Liverpool team.

But the club has to find the raw talents to start with — i.e. those talents need to exist, they cannot be made. Meanwhile, buying other English players is always an expensive gamble (Darren Bent for virtually the same price as Torres? What mad world is this?)

Should quotas be put in place, the price of England's best players will double. Unfortunately, so will that of its worst.

Liverpool have to look for the most gifted footballers at any age — those starting out as kids, to those fully established as internationals — and bring them to the club. They have to find players good enough to be ready to play alongside Jamie Carragher and Steven Gerrard now, and kids who are good enough to develop and eventually do the same.

It is only right that the system should make the best young home-grown talents *prove* they have what it takes to succeed, while the worst are let go. If the best English kids train and play regularly with the best overseas players, then they will learn from them, and they will also see what standards they have to aspire to.

If English 16- and 17-year-olds at Liverpool aren't as good as Bruna, Simon, Ajdarevic, Hansen, Pacheco and Poure, then they can have no complaints. And if they aspire to be as good, then they have to work hard at their game. It's the same for any 20-year-old: if he is not as good as Lucas or Babel, how can he complain?

Let's be clear: it's in no-one's interest if substandard local or English lads are in the Liverpool team simply because of a quota system.

It will make the football worse, and hamper the Reds' chances of success at home and in Europe (and subsequently damage the national team, the very entity this policy could conceivably be brought in to protect).

If the English Champions League teams struggle because their sides suddenly aren't as good, then the best English players will not be getting the kind of experience that has benefited the twenty-or -so to play in the semi-final or final (and some more than once) in the last four seasons.

Look at the names: Gerrard, Carragher, Crouch, Pennant, Rooney, Scholes, Neville, Terry, Lampard, Joe Cole, Ashley Cole, Campbell, Ferdinand, Wright-Phillips, Bridge, Brown.

Nearly all of these players didn't just feature in Champions League runs, they were key players. Jermaine Pennant can't get a cap for England, but was Man of the Match in a Champions League Final.

How can they be so good for their clubs in Europe, often against far better opposition than England play (Andorra, Macedonia, Russia and Croatia aren't anywhere near as talented as AC Milan or Barcelona), but so poor for England? How can they be so good in the Premiership, which is a competitive, multi-cultural league?

Could it in part be down to their clubs' non-English managers, who are among the best in the world? (Which Steve McLaren clearly isn't, and was more of a last-resort appointment.) And could it also be down to the foreign players who, when dovetailing with the locals, are so good they elevate their teams?

Everyone is talking about Scotland doing so well, but there's far more English talent out there. Even now, many of those Scottish players are Premiership reserves at best. So maybe it's not the talent, but something else that runs from the top to the bottom of the FA.

What a quota system would do would be to forcibly promote more average English players to the first team, in the hope that they develop when given the experience to do so. It would be designed to give the nation more to choose from, but would arguably just produce greater quantity and less quality. For me, the right to play in the Liverpool team should be earned, not given because of nationality.

No offence to John Welsh, Jon Otsemobor, Neil Mellor, David Raven, Zak Whitbread and Darren Potter, all of whom are fine pros (who may yet one day make it as top-division players), but they didn't prove they were good enough to be regulars for Liverpool. They didn't even come close. *[At the age of just 24, Welsh, the former England U21 international and once tipped to be a regular at Anfield, is on loan from Hull City at bottom division Chester City.]*

No home-grown player released by Liverpool in the last 15 years has gone on to look like they should have instead been a regular at Anfield. I'd much rather have Alonso, Mascherano, Reina, Arbeloa, Agger and Torres than the aforementioned players. Perhaps the difference is that, with the exception of Arbeloa, all of these looked ready for the top at 19/20.

Meanwhile, any Liverpool player currently out on loan has to take the chance to learn, develop his game, and be prepared to work hard upon his return to Liverpool, and not to think he's 'made it'. At no time can he take his eye off the ball and relax his standards.

If these players are still not ready, they have to be prepared to go back on loan, to a better club in a higher division, to maintain that gradual improvement; after all, upon their return they will be competing with players who've been to World Cups and played in Champions League finals.

I often hear 'throw the kids in, what harm can it do?', and then if the kids make a mistake, as Carson did last night, they're quickly crucified. While Carson merited the start based on his club form, it was arguably not the correct circumstances in which to give him his competitive debut; the proverbial lamb to the slaughter. He looked nervous, and who can blame him? I was nervous for him.

Pressure is a big thing in football. Pressure and confidence are two of the biggest factors in determining any given performance, often more so than talent. And youngsters have to learn to cope with the pressure and to deal with dips in confidence.

As Scott Carson has found, playing for Charlton is easier than playing for Aston Villa, and playing for Aston Villa is easier than playing for Liverpool. But playing for Charlton helped Carson step up a level to play for Villa. It was a stepping stone.

However, with Pepe Reina — who was already playing for Barcelona at 18 — so supreme between the sticks at Anfield, he was never going to get much playing time for Liverpool.

And so Carson has stepped up another level in terms of pressure in starting a crucial match for his country. It will all benefit him in the long term, providing he's allowed to forget last night (all players make mistakes, after all). But as one of England's finest keepers, and a great prospect, he is as yet nowhere near the level of Reina, who himself is still a very young keeper.

While I doubt they will be forthcoming in doing so, the English tabloids from the late '80s onwards needs to take a big share of the blame for the nation's failings.

The way they turned the England job from an already difficult position into a trial by personal ridicule, starting with Bobby Robson and reaching a nadir with Graham Taylor, was scandalous. It moved well beyond the necessary levels of criticism, and started a football-wide bandwagon of disrespecting players and managers to unacceptable degrees.

This is why I fight a lot of the media's treatment of Liverpool managers. If people can't see how the press generates pressure and damages reputations, then they only need to look at what has happened to the England managers whose heads were turned into various root vegetables.

Generally speaking, Liverpool fans are far more discerning and intelligent, but once a media perception of a manager is in place it's notoriously hard to shift.

This kind of reporting only baits the fans to further damage their own team's hopes, to the point where you have England fans in consecutive games booing Frank Lampard, their own player of the year in recent seasons, and for what? — for nothing more than not being at his best. How is that going to help one of the country's better players reproduce his form?

Two years ago you had Crouch being vociferously booed when coming on to the pitch, and for what? — for not being considered good enough for England, by 'intelligent' fans who were so accurate in that assessment they have since seen him score 14 goals in 15 starts for his country. Perhaps those fans ended up with the performances they deserved from the rest of the national team.

If Scott Carson is feeling down in the dumps today, he need only have a chat with Peter Crouch: a man who has suffered some of the worst stick imaginable, but who has come through the other side and proved himself on the international stage.

If every English kid had Crouch's attitude to go with such fine technique, the World Cup would indeed be 'coming home'.

Ten reasons for league optimism in 2005/06
13th June 2005

However realistic it may be, the start of every season brings the same dream for Liverpool fans: to win one of the 'big two' trophies. 2005 was the first time in 15 years that the dream of landing either the league title or the European Cup actually came true. I am almost certain that we will see a reversal of Liverpool's fortunes next season: an improvement domestically, while failing to retain the European Cup. Perhaps that's totally obvious: it is hard to believe Liverpool could again be as bad in the league, or as successful in Europe. But there are a fair few reasons to believe the improvement in the Premiership will be significant.

1. In the second half of the season, Liverpool will more than likely have just the league to concentrate on
If winning the Champions League once is unbelievable, retaining it would be beyond comprehension. Let's face it, it's just not going to happen, right? Chances are that this time we'll be a more rounded team, but come unstuck either unluckily, or against a superior side who, for once, we cannot beat. Certainly we can't use the underdog status a second year running. We are up there to be beaten, and six qualifying games provide extra banana skins.

I see the quarter-finals as our most realistic final destination, and I'd be more than happy with that. As a result of an earlier elimination, there will be more chance to 'concentrate on the league'. The World Club Championship won't help the fixture list, but at least it's out of the way before Christmas.

2. Everton will finish lower in the table
Just as I don't expect Liverpool to repeat the Champions League success, I fail to see how Everton can have anywhere near as good a season in the league next year. Last season, with Everton having their best season for donkey's years, the Blues' long-held position above the stuttering Reds made Benítez' task harder. Any other side looking down from 4th place would have been less of an 'issue'. Getting 4th place became a grudge match, and Liverpool had the pressing

issue of major games against Juventus and Chelsea to contend with.

There is more pressure and expectation on Everton than 12 months ago. They now have Europe to sap their energy. However, if they do repeat their success, I will take them a lot more seriously as an up-and-coming side, and not a one season wonder.

Uefa, in relenting to allow Liverpool into the Champions League, will now set in stone the regulation that 4th place is subject to the winners finishing outside the top four, in which case the reigning champions clearly deserve inclusion. All the hoopla surrounding the whole issue never helped Liverpool's cause either: Everton were in the box seat when the FA made its illogical conclusion in April.

3. The refereeing can't be as bad again, surely?

I know this is always seen as a tame argument. But if any team, big or small, doesn't get the decisions it has 'earned' with its football, then it can struggle. When it has a new manager, and new players, it's so crucial to get off to a good start.

The second half of the season was pretty non-eventful in terms of bad refereeing either for or against Liverpool in the Premiership. Chelsea on New Year's Day, and the two penalties the Reds were never awarded, was the turning point. There were one or two debatable decisions after that game, but nothing major. The usual 'par for the course' stuff.

But a collection of outrageously poor decisions in the first half of the season stopped Liverpool getting a better foothold in the league table. A good start to the season sets the tone, and it was notable that key decisions went against the Reds in the first two away games: Steven Gerrard clearly fouled in the box at White Hart Lane on the opening day, in a game that was eventually drawn; and a great Luis Garcia goal wrongly chalked off at the Reebok — a defeat that would have become a draw. That was potentially four points'-worth of poor decisions in the first weeks of the season alone.

Had those decisions been correctly awarded in the Reds' favour, there is every chance the Reds would have built some momentum on the road. Instead, Liverpool couldn't buy a win away from Anfield, and the league campaign never really got out of second gear.

4. Rafa now knows the Premiership better, and knows more about opposition teams and players

Much of Rafa's success in Spain was down to analysing the opposition, with the help of Pako Ayestaran, to the *nth* degree. The pair were famed for pinpointing the weaknesses in every team, and utilising different tactics, players and styles of play to exploit them.

This time around, not only will Rafa and Pako better understand the demands of English football, they will know how all the other teams like to set out their stall, and what players are dangerous (as well as those whose weaknesses can be taken advantage of). It stands to reason that our management will be better equipped this time around.

Liverpool could have gone for an English manager in 2004 who might have managed, given that he will have had a deep knowledge of the league, to get an extra ten points in the league last season, but who would have had no experience in Europe. And those extra ten points might have proved the best any English manager could manage — as good as it gets; Benítez has league titles under his belt. He has shown he can win a major league, not once but twice.

Great managers tend to improve their side's results year-by-year, certainly for the first three or four years. So next season should see a marked domestic improvement.

5. Last season's new signings will be more used to the Premiership

For a man who was too lightweight for the Premiership, eight league goals from open play (and two legitimate ones at Bolton and Boro wrongly chalked off) wasn't a bad return for Luis Garcia. Of these ten 'goals', five were away — where he was supposed to be anonymous. But it's clear he still has room for improvement, and if he is surrounded by better players than last season he will find more freedom and space.

Although Xabi Alonso adjusted particularly well, at times the games seemed a little too frantic for him — especially when Gerrard wasn't in the team to distract the opposition. Alonso is only just 23, so the potential is massive — he will get better as a player, and better as a *Premiership* footballer.

The main benefactors should be Fernando Morientes and Djibril Cissé, neither of whom started even one-third of last season's league matches: Cissé starting only ten league games, Morientes 12. They've had a good taste of the Premiership, and next season should see them reap the rewards. Cissé appeared to be coming to terms with the nature of the pace of the game here in the final home match against Aston Villa — although his statement that he 'didn't want the season to end' seems to have been taken rather too literally by Uefa. He will be extremely hungry and determined to make up for lost time, starting early next month.

6. New signings

Not all of Rafa's summer signings will settle quickly and effectively, but the chances are that at least half will. If one of those signings is Pepe Reina, the Villareal 'keeper, then he has to settle almost immediately — one area of the team where you can't afford an extended period of acclimatisation is between the sticks. If you list the areas where the squad is a little lacking, there could be a fair few additions: two strikers, two midfielders, two defenders and a goalkeeper.

Of those leaving, none will be too sorely missed — unlike Owen, who left last summer. (Unless, of course, Gerrard does end up packing his bags.) Players like Biscan and Smicer played their best games for the club in Europe; their league form was never consistent enough, and of course Baros never quite hit the heights he promised. That's why even half-decent Premiership players (if they are effective) might help bolster the squad with regards to the domestic programme, although of course we want the best players possible — or rather, the best *blend* possible.

7. The 'big guns' will be fit

Or at least we hope they will. An injury-free season from Steven Gerrard, Xabi Alonso and Djibril Cissé will be like three new top-class signings. Add all the other players who missed too much football last year (Hamann, Kewell, Kirkland, Sinama-Pongolle, Nunez, Mellor), and you have an entire team of players unavailable to Rafa for much of last season.

8. Emerging talent

There's not much to crow about — no outrageously talented youngsters on the horizon, destined for world superstardom — but in John Welsh, Darren Potter, David Raven, Zak Whitbread, Carl Medjani, Anthony Le Tallec and Sinama-Pongolle, the club has a very fine collection of 20/21 year-olds, all of whom picked up valuable first team experience last season. That includes Medjani at L'Orient — the youngster just captained France to the U20 Toulon championship, in case anyone thinks he's average because he hasn't yet broken into the Liverpool first team.

Expect Rafa to sign some youngsters for the future, but one or two might be able to add something to the team sooner rather than later. Even Alou Diarra — now a fully fledged French international — might return, especially now Biscan has been released. He will report for pre-season training like all other Reds, unless he is loaned out once again, or sold.

9. Liverpool will be firmly into the groove by the time the Premiership kicks in

Pre-season matches are handy, but nothing beats competitive games. Not only did Liverpool's season end 10 days after the Premiership concluded, but the club's season will start a whole month before the league resumes. That's nearly six weeks of added fitness. The Reds will now be able to enjoy a nice couple of weeks' holiday, but won't have time to lose too much conditioning.

The worry is that the team will 'hit the wall' in the new year. But it's always better to have points in the bag, as we saw with Everton this season. A good start to the season breeds confidence, and suddenly you find yourselves on a 'run'. That has to be the hope. A good start to the league campaign will reinforce the idea that Liverpool are actually now a very special side under Benítez. Even if that's still not 100% true, and the side remains essentially one in transition, a good start will give the impression of an unstoppable force.

10. What better place to end than this: Liverpool FC, Champions of Europe?

Winning one of the 'big two' tells the players of the levels they can achieve. Once you've climbed Everest you can do so again. While the success was in Europe, the *confidence* will be 'transferable'. The cup success of 2001 enabled the club to do better in the Premiership in 2002, finishing 2nd with 80 points.

2001/02 did not follow a transitional season. But unlike then, this time Liverpool achieved something where they could say they were 'the best'. The Uefa Cup is for those deemed inferior in the first place; the Champions League is for *the best teams only*. According to the name engraved on this season's cup, Liverpool are the 'best of the best'.

It wasn't just winning the Champions League, it was the manner in which it was achieved. Nothing will ever feel like a 'lost cause' again. If you can beat some great teams on the way to the final, and then come back from 3-0 down at half-time to AC Milan in the biggest club game on the planet, you can come back against *anyone*. [*As the Reds would subsequently prove, with a thrilling comeback against, erm, Luton.*] It doesn't mean that you will, of course: but the players now know that anything is possible.

That is a powerful psychological boost in football that can be worth a lot of points over the course of a season. Half of the battle takes place in the players' minds, and their minds should be filled with the idea of *possibilities*.

Liverpool ended the season with 82 points and the FA Cup.

An Open Letter to George Gillett and Tom Hicks

November 26th 2007

Dear George and Tom,

I'd just like to express how depressed and upset I am by the continuing uncertainty surrounding the club, and I'd love to hear some reassurances that the differences will be settled ASAP — and that Rafa Benítez has your full support and backing.

While I do think there are two sides to any story, and I appreciate the difficulties of running any club (balancing the books, keeping fans happy, and dealing with opinionated, strong-minded individuals), what I've heard these past few days leads me increasingly to believe you might be missing the point regarding football transfers, and in so doing, undermining the manager, whether you meant to or not.

You may not have realised, perhaps through cultural differences, that telling a manager of an English football team to 'just coach the side' is a kind of insult.

I am not about to make accusations, or go on some personal tirade against you both, particularly with a welter of hearsay and little actual hard evidence (as yet) fuelling the media frenzy. Clearly all is not well, but at the same time, is it all 'lost'?

I just want to know that the club I love is in safe hands; I feel that is the case on the pitch, but that's something relatively easy to assess; assessing how a club is being run behind the scenes from our side of the fence is much more difficult, because we don't get to see what happens, and only hear snippets of information which is often wrapped up in rumour and hearsay.

I felt Rafa's tone after the Newcastle game was fairly conciliatory, in saying you had the best interests of the club at heart, and that as you were new you needed time to settle into the roles — like he'd expect with a new player. You are no strangers to running sports teams, but you cannot match Rafa's knowledge when it comes to football. Few men can. In this sense, you are the rookies, and you would surely acknowledge that.

And if it is indeed true that you don't (yet) fully understand how the transfer system in Europe works, then it seems to me that this needs to be remedied as soon as possible. This is a fundamental basic of the game. I would like to think it's a misunderstanding, and that there's been some transatlantic miscommunication. I hope I'm not being naive in holding out some hope that this is the case.

Also, I understood that Foster Gillett was going to be acting as your eyes, ears and the in-house go-between in Liverpool, but reports suggest that he is not in place?

For the record, I can't think of one successful English club which has chopped and changed its managers, and which hasn't given the man in charge of the team full control. A club like Newcastle United has become a laughing stock because of this short-sighted approach. Continuity and stability are paramount to football success.

There have been some woeful attempts at Director of Football-type affairs, and the only time I know that this type of arrangement has worked was when David Dein bought players at Arsenal, but — crucially — at Arsene Wenger's behest.

Across North London, Spurs — whose net spend this summer was greater than Liverpool's (as was Manchester United's and Manchester City's) — were spectacularly undone by the appointment of a Technical Director whose views differed from the manager's. Too many cooks with different ideas ...

I understand a natural fear you might have — that of sensing the head of the team possesses too much power — but English football works this way. You need one man with one vision to hold the wheel and steer the ship; not rule by committee. And he needs to be so much more than just a 'coach'.

Any manager worth his salt a) will be wary of working for a club that does not give him full power in all football matters, and b) will likely be as difficult a character as Benítez, if not more so. Neutering a manager is never the answer.

Top managers are not easy men to work with. Ferguson, Mourinho, Shankly, Clough — none made life easy for the board, and none took kindly to being told what to do, but each delivered the goods in the end. Arsene Wenger is the same, although he was able to build his Arsenal empire with the full backing of David Dein. Had he been told otherwise, he would not have hung around.

Please note what Arsene Wenger said this week: "Maybe there is an analysis to do about politics in the modern [managerial] game. Benítez has done remarkably well and certainly what's happening at Liverpool is not down to the sport or to results, it's down to other, internal differences. Apparently, there are differences. I have always had the support of my board and I think [Sir Alex] Ferguson had that [at Manchester United] as well, and we are the longest-serving managers in the league. There's no secret in it.

"They [the Arsenal board] understand that there is no success without that but, of course, you need a bit of experience to understand that and I'm not sure that everybody just coming and buying [clubs] understands that. The only thing I can say is that I have had the freedom to work since I arrived at Arsenal. I can't remember my board saying 'No' to me."

Stability is key for any successful club. Rafa Benítez is doing far, far, far better at this stage of his tenure than Alex Ferguson was at United. You cannot imagine how much better he is doing. Ferguson failed to win a trophy until the end of his 4th season, and his average league position after five seasons was a woeful 9th. His finishes were 11th, 13th, 2nd, 13th and 6th. Compare this with 5th, 3rd, 3rd, plus an FA Cup and two Champions League Finals, one of which was so famously won, and you can see the chasm.

Replacing Rafa now, when he has assembled his best squad and had his best league start, really would make no sense to me — win the game in hand and the Reds would be 2nd, and still unbeaten by the start of December. The team is set up to work to his methods. The players fit his mould. And from what I can tell, they have the utmost respect for him. This is crucial.

And while I do think there are perhaps a handful of managers in football who are in the same league as Rafa, I do not think their methods are necessarily suited to Liverpool FC, and I definitely don't think they could make as much of this particular squad as Rafa can. They would want to bring in their own new players, which would be costly, and introduce new systems, which would put things back. And one of those managers, Arsene Wenger, already has a job he's happy with, free from interference.

In terms of money spent, Benítez's overall transfer record is outstanding. All managers make mistakes, but most of his have been cheap ones who were quickly traded. What he has got for his money has been top-rate. The squads of United and Chelsea cost at least twice as much as Liverpool's, and are full of £15-£30m players, yet is there really much of a gap in class? Meanwhile, Arsenal are making use of young players they procured many years ago.

Fan opinion is almost exclusively siding with Rafa. While there has also been some unhelpful, xenophobic anti-American rhetoric, which just clouds the issue, you need to understand how unpopular this situation is making you amongst the Anfield faithful, and how high spirits are running.

When you took over the club there was a surprising amount of goodwill. I don't mean surprising in that at the time that I felt you deserved anything less, but surprising in that any new owners could perhaps have expected a rougher ride. As fans it seems our patience had been worn down with almost three years without a solution to the investment issue, and a series of desperately unsuitable suitors chancing their arms. Compared with Thaksin Shinawatra, you seemed like Mother Teresa (with money).

Maybe there are very valid reasons, and I will try to keep as open a mind as possible, but I am struggling to know why the matter cannot be discussed and an attempt at resolving it made before the 16th December, in three weeks' time.

I have to admit that such a delay worries me. The issues at hand — be they laying the foundations for transfers well ahead of the window (as all teams do), or repairing the relationship with Rafa — seem rather too pressing for that. I don't see how they can wait.

If failure to get through the league stage of the Champions League is crucial to the financial planning for the transfer window, I can understand that part of your thinking. On the other hand, if it is crucial as to whether or not Benítez is fired, I cannot understand that for one minute. Before Rafa was here, we weren't even qualifying for the competition, let alone reaching two finals.

Rafa spoke out after Athens, but you seemed to understand his frustrations. You went on to help the club secure some fantastic players over the summer, although the net spend — while healthy — was not remarkable. One further £7m target — Gabriel Heinze — was missed very late in the day, so it's clear from the summer that such a defender was needed, while any manager will always be assessing his squad as to how he can strengthen it. They do not rest, either on their laurels, or just literally, it seems.

Having spent the past three years studiously observing Rafa's methods, I've come to realise just how good he is. I believe he is a football visionary, and what he is building at Liverpool will be something really special.

For instance, it's now seven months since we conceded a goal from a corner or free-kick delivered into the box (excluding the 'reserve' team fielded in the Carling Cup). Zonal marking was widely mocked in 2004, and now we see other teams conceding lame goals with man-to-man marking every week. It's just one area where Rafa made a controversial change, stuck with it in the face of criticism, and now is reaping the rewards.

My instincts tell me that you are too smart to dispense with a man like Rafa, and that for all the tension you do really respect him. My instincts tell me you have too much to lose, in terms of talent, squad morale, financial resources and fan backing, by making such a drastic move — if, indeed, that is what you are considering.

If one good thing has come of this, it's that it's made the fans unite behind the manager and his team. The fear of losing Rafa, which may be just paper talk but all the same seems very real to many fans, has made the faithful realise just what it is they have to be grateful for.

So, please reassure me, and all other nervous Reds, that it's all one big (unfortunate) misunderstanding, and that yourselves, Rick Parry and Rafa can get together for a group hug sooner rather than later. I'll even buy the coffee and donuts.

Identifying with the players
Unpublished, 2006

I think it's fair to say that I don't exactly identify with many modern footballers. I've never liked the music of Phil Collins, or had a burning desire to appear in *OK! Magazine*. I've never been one for bling (although the chance to have the fortunes to waste on it would be a fine thing), and the only dogging I've been party to involved walking my border collie around the park.

But I do think I understand a lot of what it's like to be a player. The ability to empathise is one of the essential traits of any writer, but you also need a grounding in the subject. Not enough football writers have much actual playing experience to draw from, to aid that understanding; they might be great journalists, or talented writers, but there can be a lack of insight into the thought processes of a footballer in any given situation. And the footballers who become writers aren't always the most insightful. Or intelligible. And that's if they're not merely hiding behind the facade of a ghost writer.

My own playing experiences were at a lower level, but it was competitive all the same. The club's ground had a stand, and a clubhouse. And floodlights, albeit ones constructed around the time electricity was first invented. FA-appointed referees and linesmen officiated. People had to pay to watch me. (Not that anyone handed over money to specifically see me. I'm sure some would have paid extra to ensure my absence.) And some weeks I got paid, too. I played in the qualifying rounds of the FA Cup.

As a result, I can relate to a lot of the problems players face: confidence crises; playing with injuries, and how difficult that can be when everyone else is physically fit and sharp; going up a level or two in terms of the standard of football, and how long it can take to adapt; trying to convince a manager, and, for that matter, team-mates, of your worth; indeed, convincing yourself you have what it takes, and fighting your own doubts. It's just a question of extrapolating those experiences onto a higher stage. There was relatively little pressure on me, but there was the pressure I put on myself; the games I played were important to me, as was my performance. I've been the star player in a mediocre team, and the worst player in a very good team, before I eventually became one of the better (if not the best) players in that very good team. I've had supreme confidence, and zero confidence.

When footballers break into the first team, move to a big club like Liverpool, or experience acclaim in early internationals, there's the rush of adrenaline, and the boost to confidence. Being on an upward curve has a self-sustaining life of its own. For a while, at least. But then it eventually levels off. The novelty diminishes, and dissatisfaction creeps in. Just getting into the Liverpool team for a ten-minute run out in the Carling Cup, which might have meant the world to a young Academy starlet, is no longer 'new'. It's no longer enough. He wants to get a first Premiership bow. Then, when that's achieved, a regular berth. To go from the giddy highs of a run-out under the floodlights of a packed house at Anfield, to the 'one man and his dog' crowd at a low-key reserve fixture, must be demoralising.

The most successful people in life, and in sport, get to a level, and then they strive to do better. They are not the sort of people who say "Right, I've done that, I can put my feet up".

I can see why both Michael Owen and Steven Gerrard felt restless at Liverpool in 2004. Sometimes you need a new challenge, in order to stop standing still, which, like a pond, leads to stagnation. The trouble with Gerrard in 2004 was possibly that he felt he could play no better in a Liverpool shirt, while the team itself was deteriorating; and a year later, that he could take the club no higher, having lifted the European Cup.

Or perhaps it was just the desire to be wanted? To feel special? To get some kind of boost that was otherwise not forthcoming? It's one thing to be offered a pay rise by a club; it's another to have that club tying itself in knots to keep you. Or indeed, to have another club coming in for you, willing to pay an immense fee and obscene wages. It must give you a thrill, and turn your head. For players, the wage packet can be as much about status, and a sense of value, than how many small countries can be bought with it.

The challenge for a player like Steven Gerrard is to re-motivate himself every season, without a change of surroundings. It's easy to say we'd never leave Liverpool, if we were so lucky as to be good enough to be in that position, as simply playing for the club would be the realisation of our wildest fantasies (ignoring those involving Jennifer Love Hewitt and whipped cream). But if we had earned the right to get to that point, we'd probably feel that restlessness too.

For me it's about trying to understand the 'human' elements that go on with players. They are not robots. Ultimately the best players should be able to find their way, and overcome any problems, provided they are given enough time. Very few world-class players suffer inexorably; they tend to all come good before too long. But that's just a small percentage of the players out there; most teams rely on a collection of merely 'very good' players, and they are the ones that can be dragged down to the level of mediocre by problems such as settling into a new country, adapting to a new team, and all the other challenges associated with a new club or a new country; not to mention what is going on in their personal lives that can have such a massive bearing on their state of mind. Some may play football to escape their problems, and revel in those 90 minutes of total immersion, but others will take their worries onto the pitch with them. While they may not be directly thinking about their wife having an affair or their ill young child or parent while going into a 50-50 with John Terry whose studs are showing, it may be affecting their ability to sleep at night, or stay focused in training, and all that is then transferred into the match itself.

Fans get angry at players they see as under-performing, or not pulling their weight. I often see the comparisons made with a footballer doing his job (or not, as the accusation tends to be) and a fan's working life, sometimes from manual labourers. I'm not belittling such professions (my father was a sheet metal worker), but working unbelievably hard — even somewhere as harsh and unglamorous as down a coal mine — involves a totally different kind of pressure. You have a job to do, and your family to feed. The working conditions may be far from pleasant, and there may be safety issues. It's tough. And of course, your work will be monitored. But it will not be scrutinised to the *nth* degree by up to a billion people at times. You clock on, you clock off, and put in a solid shift in between. And while someone like Jerzy Dudek will have a greater sense of perspective, and be more appreciative of his good fortune having looked set for a career in the pits of Silesia in Poland, that good fortune wouldn't have felt so special when he allowed Diego Forlan to score at Anfield. In those moments there is nowhere to hide. We'd all rather be footballers than miners. But that doesn't mean it's an easy, straightforward existence. While miners will dream of the luxury lifestyle of the successful footballer, there will be times when someone like Dudek wishes a hole, like those dark pits in Silesia, had swallowed him up. Perhaps one of the hardest things for footballers to cope with is the inability to escape their work. A bad day at the office follows them everywhere they go: on the tv, internet, in newspapers, and out at the supermarket or a quiet bar/restaurant. It's not about pitying footballers their lot. Just understanding that it is not always easy to go out and put on your best display. The mental pressures are pretty unique, with little escape in a goldfish bowl world.

Football is not about doing a job; such comparisons cannot be made. It's about *performing*. It's about excelling week after week, no matter how you feel, no matter what your mood or what is going on in your personal life. (Was it any coincidence that Dirk Kuyt's performances dipped around the time his father had an operation for cancer?)

It's more like being a rock star or an actor, in that you have to go out and wow people. Fans actually don't want to see players going out and doing a job; they want to see them doing a great job, giving it their all, with their heart and their souls. But even rock stars know the words to the songs; actors follow a script. So maybe it's more like improvisational theatre or comedy: you have to stand in front of a crowd that demands to be impressed, and you are winging it, flying by the seat of your pants. It's an off-the-cuff profession, and it can easily go wrong, especially if there's a bad start to proceedings.

For a start, no one is setting out to stop you do your job. Try assembling your particular section in a Vauxhall car factory with employees from the Ford factory literally putting a spanner in the works. You look around, and your colleagues are not really helping you out as they should be. They're having an off day. You are relying on them, but they are having their own problems. And rather than assemble the engine to set plans, you have to make it up as go along; you have vague instructions, but colleagues aren't handing you the right parts at the right times. Football isn't a sport like golf or darts where you only have to concentrate on your own game, and hitting certain targets. You compete against an opponent, but you are free to swing your club or throw your arrows. Football is an incredibly complex sport in a number of ways, made all the more so by the attention it gets, in both the front and back pages.

It's never my intention to be too critical of players who aren't performing well, because I understand how form, fitness and confidence (and all its related mental conditions) go hand-in-hand. I know how easy it is to look ten times worse than you really are, and how, once the tide turns, you can suddenly pull the odd bit of magic out of the hat and have no idea where it came from. So long as a player is trying, then he needs to be supported.

But at times it can be hard to even tell if someone is indeed trying, because when things are going wrong a stiltedness comes into a player's game; an awkwardness, a clumsiness. Over-thinking overtakes intuitive movement; rather than act quickly and decisively, he can find himself caught in two minds, and rooted to the spot as each option is reviewed. Fear starts to a play a paralysing role. Some players have a natural bullishness that sees them through dips in form; others — usually the flair players — find themselves naturally shrinking after every poorly executed trick.

That said, there will always be players who shirk responsibility and who become more interested in the wage packet, nights on the town and ostentatious jewellery, than the the kind of bling we want to see draped around their necks: shiny new medals presented in May. But it's not always easy to spot the difference between a player struggling for confidence and a player who has lost interest. And it can be difficult for players to go out for a quiet, relaxing meal or drink, given their celebrity. (Equally, some players are their own worst enemies when it comes to their choice of nightspot.)

If a player has proven to the fans that he's top quality (for example, Xabi

Alonso), then it's easy to say class is permanent and form temporary; if he hasn't proven it, it doesn't mean he won't. A certain benefit of the doubt is essential to let a player flourish; turning on him after two games is going to be counter-productive. But there has to be a time limit, some kind of cut-off point where you say enough is enough. Morientes is a case in point. In his third season he might have finally shown the form we expected (i.e. the form he showed once he returned to Spain with Valencia); but the likelihood was greatly diminished with each passing year. Who honestly believed he was suddenly going to come good in English football, especially as, at 30, he wasn't getting any younger? And 18 months of 'failure' becomes an expanding weight to bear. However, shipping him out in June 2005, after a disappointing initial six months, would have been premature. There hadn't been enough time for him to adapt, and if a player is not allowed a period of adaptation then he is effectively hamstrung. Too many of the league's top players took six months to settle: the most obvious examples are always Thierry Henry and Robert Pires, two recent Footballers of the Year who initially stunk out Highbury.

A similar attitude was needed with Morientes and Cissé: judging too quickly would mean not giving them time to come into their own. They had enough pedigree to suggest success was possible. You had to hope, and trust, that they'd come good. Ultimately they didn't, but by then they had been given the chance. Had Arsene Wenger been as impatient with Thierry Henry as were Juventus, for whom he only played 16 times, then one of the best-ever players to grace English football could have found himself back in France, never to again be trusted by anyone from the big leagues. His core confidence — on which so much of his strutting brilliance relies — could have been irreparably damaged. Perhaps it's unlikely that someone so gifted would stay out of the headlines for long, but it's not implausible. Plenty of other prodigious talents have found themselves making the wrong move at the wrong time in their careers, and from being the next-best thing found themselves endlessly struggling to rediscover their 'mojo'. Once careers take a downturn, if it's not rectified fairly quickly it can lead to a downward spiral, as their careers corkscrew into oblivion. (Or West Bromich Albion.)

While Cissé may not have been given the chance he felt he needed — i.e. to play up front 50 games a season — he was at least given enough time by Benítez for the manager himself to decide if he fitted his own needs or not. It wasn't like shipping the 34-year-old Pellegrino out after five difficult months; that old dog was never going to learn enough new tricks, especially in a league where greyhounds are the norm, and where a career, to conclude the metaphor, had gone to the dogs. Cissé had his chance, and at least we now know that under Benítez's style of play and type of man-management, the

Frenchman was never going to feel at ease enough to flourish. The Dutchman Dirk Kuyt was more to Benítez's liking.

But Kuyt had his own struggles off the pitch after arriving in England. After a good start, his form seemed to dip. He got two goals in his first few games, but then went five games without scoring. Then it became known that his father had undergone surgery for cancer back in Holland. Kuyt Snr, unsteady on his feet, presented his son with the Dutch Footballer of the Year at the ceremony while recuperating after the operation, and then a couple of weeks later finally flew over to England to watch his son play. Kuyt Jnr promptly broke his mini-drought with a superb strike against Aston Villa, and followed it up with two more a week later. It may have been coincidental, but it's hard to believe that a parent undergoing life-saving surgery several hundred miles away wouldn't have had a bearing on a player's struggles on the pitch. And to that end I can empathise.

But perhaps Dirk Kuyt is a good example to end on, having started with a dig at the expense of those footballers who choose to spend their money on needless accessories and live excessively shallow existences. In the Dutchman the Reds have signed a decent human being. It would be nice to be able to identify more with footballers, and have them be as grounded as possible; in touch with the common man. You sense some are like that; it's hard to imagine Jamie Carragher 'giving it large' and acting the 'big I am', but others seem to live in their ivory towers. (Then again, with people's often abusive attitudes to celebrities, and the hounding they can receive in public, it may be the safest place for some of them.)

Kuyt's grounding at Quick Boys at Katwijk, on the Dutch coast, serves him well to this day. Players who come up the hard way — who don't feel like superstars at the age of 11 when a big club signs them on — tend to appreciate their success all the more. The son of a sailor, he learned the game in a town when amateur football was serious business, and the game was based on guts rather than the more traditional Dutch flair (no wonder Kuyt considers his style 'English'). But he continued to take his game more seriously than the professionals he would later play with and against as he rose through Dutch football, heading to Utrecht at 18 and then onto Feyenoord at 22, with neither team totally convinced of his quality when signing him. His spare time was spent either in the gym, with a physiotherapist or visiting a sports psychologist. He worked that bit harder, and got his due rewards.

But even then, once he made the big time and became the star of his country's league, he never acted with anything other than humility. When Kuyt told Dutch football writer Simon Kuper that, "I must thank God on my bare knees that I became a footballer" he really means it. Much of his earnings are put towards charitable work. And while it's none of my business what any football spends his own money on, it's always easier to respect someone who knows what it's like in the real world. And with that I can most definitely identify.

'Golden Past, Red Future' Revisited

Unpublished essay from November 2006, with 2008 updates in brackets.

When, in the winter of 2004, I set about the task of writing *Golden Past, Red Future* (with the able assistance of Jonathan Swain), I did not expect it to still be selling six weeks after its release, let alone the number one football book, and still in the Amazon Top 10 football chart over a year later. In truth, I wasn't even sure it would make it into print — like embarking on a voyage with no definite destination, I set off with hope but no masterplan as to where I expected it to take me. And, of course, I had no idea on what kind of journey the team was about to embark upon, in what were still very uncertain days for Benítez's men.

Had I known then what I know now, I might have been scared of putting so many opinions into the book, and instead stuck with a more straightforward factual assessment. So it's probably for the best that I was blissfully oblivious, in spite of any subsequent flaws that can be traced with the aid of hindsight.

The trouble with expressing opinions in print is that they can date very quickly. You are tied into thoughts that may well have seemed true at the time, but which have subsequently changed. There are a few paragraphs that I'd cut out of every copy if I could, and I'd Tippex out a few further sentences. But that's all what I felt at the time, for better or for worse.

As the book was starting to take shape, in January 2005, there was a maelstrom of criticism of the club, from top to bottom. Parry, Moores, Benítez, and almost every player came in for scathing attacks, and I had to wonder what the hell I'd be documenting. Results were bad. The defeat at Southampton, orchestrated by Peter Crouch, was a pretty dire performance; although it's still remarkable how anyone can say it was the worst in 40 years. Going out of the FA Cup at Burnley was another massive setback, albeit one that would turn into a mixed blessing with the fixture list as the team made it through to the latter stages of the Champions League.

Of course, with the writing of a sequel of sorts — *Red Revival* — a lot of the issues raised in the previous book were naturally addressed a year later, while *Above Us Only Sky*, from 2007, continued the process; the progress of the club followed seamlessly from one book to the next in many senses. Where possible, this piece relates to specific points that didn't crop up in *Red Revival* and *Above Us Only Sky*.

Gérard Houllier – his reputation now?

Golden Past, Red Future was written fairly soon after the departure of the man once affectionately known as Le Boss (before things turned to *merde*). Has much changed in the intervening period, now that there is some distance between the Frenchman and his time in charge? How good was his legacy, in terms of the players he left behind? And how has his reputation subsequently changed?

It remains undeniable that a large proportion of the 2005 Champions League success was built upon Houllier's foundations. 'His' players made up the majority of the 14 men Benítez called upon in Istanbul. Both Carragher and Gerrard had come of age under Houllier, with the latter instantly given his debut when Roy Evans had not seen fit to promote the Huyton youngster to the first team squad. Gerrard would have thrived without Houllier, but both of the young Liverpudlians benefited from his guidance, at a time when they most needed to be shown the right direction for a professional footballer. Of course, Houllier did not buy either player, so they are not exclusively 'his'; he was making use of two men already at the club. Eleven of the 14 players used in Istanbul were either Houllier purchases or players he groomed.

In *Golden Past, Red Future* I pointed out the successful purchases of the French manager, and there were plenty over the years. It's important to not just focus on the flops, of which the numbers were high, too. But most of Houllier's best buys were in the first half of his tenure. Of the players he signed who were part of that fifth European Cup success, few now remain. Sami Hyypia, who pound-for-pound must rate as the best bit of business Liverpool have done in many years, is nearing the winding-down period in his career, after almost 400 games for the club; but he is still an important player at 33. Steve Finnan rediscovered his form only once Houllier had been sacked, but remains a great acquisition. And Didi Hamann, who finally left Liverpool in the summer of 2006, gave the Reds full value for his £8m fee, and then some. Any manager would be proud of such acquisitions.

But after those three it starts to get a little less clear. Jerzy Dudek was the hero of Istanbul, but since 2002 his time at Liverpool, bar that one remarkable game, has been distinctly average, and since the best night of his career he's been almost exclusively a reserve keeper at the club. His exceptional first season, and his acrobatics in Turkey, prove that Houllier purchased a player of real ability; but it's how goalkeepers react to adversity and maintain their confidence that defines their careers. He'll be remembered fondly, but not as an out-and-out success.

Djimi Traoré presented a shrewd investment, given that his £500,000 fee was quadrupled seven years later when Charlton came knocking. His playing time was distinctly mixed, to put it politely, but he was a very handy squad player. Milan Baros appeared to have such a bright future in 2002, and then again after Euro 2004, but his goalscoring record remains impressive only at international level. He's yet to spark into life at Aston Villa, but remains young enough to fulfil his potential; however, it's unlikely he'll ever prove to be the truly great striker many anticipated when he was making his way at Banik Ostrava in the Czech Republic. Harry Kewell's fitness problems have made assessing his time at the club troublesome; he's not delivered anywhere near what was expected, but he's barely played when free of injuries. If he has yet to live up to his reputation, he was also acquired without a big transfer fee. Vladimir Smicer, like Dudek, wrote his name large in the history books with his contribution to the Champions League victory, but like Kewell missed too much football with injuries, and never found a rhythm to his game. The Czech was clearly a talented individual, but English football never seemed to suit him.

Djibril Cissé just didn't work out as hoped. It's an odd situation to assess, as the player was bought to play with a certain tactical approach, and the whole game-plan was changed with the arrival of Benítez. As discussed later in this chapter, Cissé had his moments. But the deficiencies to his game mean you have no choice but to question whether he'd have been a success even with a manager more attuned to his needs.

So while Houllier's signings proved capable, under the guidance of a superior tactician, of reaching incredible heights, too many were ultimately too weak or inconsistent to work their way into Benítez's long-term plans. And that's just those who were involved in Istanbul. Salif Diao, Igor Biscan, Anthony Le Tallec, Chris Kirkland and Florent Sinama-Pongolle have also departed the club in the meantime, in one form or another. Most are on long-term loans, and all could lead to permanent departures.

There was a bad aftertaste following the end of *Le Revolution*, from which it's impossible to escape. Those last two seasons cloud all assessments of Houllier's reign. Even now it's odd to recall how truly loved he was at one stage. It was strange when, in the act of preparing for this article, I went through old articles and had to read about the affection held for 'GH' in 2001, both in terms of my own admiration and that of other Reds. It's easy to forget how frequent were the comparisons with Bill Shankly, even if it's now a likeness that looks horribly ill conceived, and an insult to the founder of modern Liverpool. Houllier gave the club back its pride and desire after the wayward '90s, and in 2001 led the Reds to a kind of treble that may never be repeated. A year later it was a case of so close yet so far. But that's where the good news ended. Houllier's time was like a film that's gripping until the halfway mark, when it fails to sustain its momentum and falls horribly apart. (All it needed was a cameo from Madonna to confirm it as a bona fide turkey.)

Since the book was published Houllier has taken over at Lyon: a team that had won the French league the previous four seasons, and in that time become increasingly potent in Europe. While maintaining success at any club is never simple, such was the domination of Lyon that it's difficult to afford Houllier the fullest respect for landing the club its fifth title on the bounce; after all, he was the third manager to lead them to the title in that time, suggesting a job in which it is easy to succeed. Following success with Paris St Germain in 1986, the triumph with Lyon became Houllier's second major honour, some twenty years apart. (His role in the French World Cup win in 1998 is rightly praised, but it was only in an advisory capacity.) But what he needs to ensure a reputation as one of the greats is to do something new; take a club further than it's been before (or in the recent past) in one of the two big competitions: major European league or European Cup. Benítez achieved such feats at both Valencia, where he ended a 31-year wait for the La Liga crown, and at Liverpool, where he pulled the Champions League rabbit out of an invisible hat. It's that extra step, and no matter how many times Houllier wins the league with Lyon he won't be taking the club any further. What he needs, given his team's domestic dominance, is success in the Champions League: an historic achievement. If he does that, he will have elevated himself into the pantheon of truly great coaches.

Balance

For me, one of the more successful parts of *Golden Past, Red Future* was the section about how Rafa Benítez needed to shape his team over time, and how the continual tinkering with the personnel, as he works towards his favoured solutions, would come with a number of cons as well as pros. It remains a universal truth of football that every time something is adjusted with positive intent, either tactically or in terms of a particular player, there are going to be at least some negative consequences. No player, when introduced into the line-up, comes without any flaws. Every player put into the team means something is also taken away from the team. Unless you can find eleven perfect all-round players who also happen to understand every tactical nuance, change will mean potential drawbacks; the key is to make sure any replacement offers more additional positives than negatives. But even if the positives outweigh the negatives, it can take a player — and his team-mates — time to make sense of the new situation.

Benítez continues to seek the blend between attack and defence. The transfers in the summer of 2006 saw a new emphasis on the attacking side of the game: two quick wingers to hug the touchline and get to the byline. Where Luis Garcia and Steven Gerrard look to cut inside to get involved in play whenever stationed in wide areas, and Djibril Cissé lacked the natural instincts to be a real success in the role, the two new players would be prepared to get chalk on their boots, and enable the Reds to 'widen the pitch'. But in so doing, it would also make the midfield less defensively compact. While they perform with the Benítez work ethic in mind, neither Mark Gonzalez nor Jermaine Pennant are the kind of solid midfielders who are extremely comfortable tracking back. Rather than all-rounders (as is Gerrard in the role), they are best on the front-foot.

There has also been a switch from a lone-striker formation, which was Benítez's preferred system in his early days, into one which deploys two out-and-out forwards. At the start of Benítez's third season a more attacking philosophy was leaving more holes at the back. The search for the perfect balance was proving elusive.

Who ran over the black cat?

I'm still uncomfortable blaming bad fortune and inadequate refereeing for poor results, in that it never sounds totally credible. But it remains the case that in Benítez's first season he suffered both an injury crisis and a spate of poor decisions from the officials. The interesting thing is that his second season, when consistency was found for much of the ten months, was relatively free of major injuries, while there also seemed a fairly normal amount of poor decisions both for and against the Reds. It was a successful season in a number of ways, with the second-highest ever percentage of league games won, an excellent Champions League group stage (albeit followed by a swift exit), and the FA Cup, won in style at the expense of a number of top-flight teams along the way. But the start of his third season was again marred by poor decisions from officials.

Ultimately you have to overcome any adversity that crops up during a season. But when crucial decisions are incorrectly awarded against you, especially at key moments in games, it can adversely shape the rest of the contest. You can't always undo the damage to confidence, and the psychological blow, even with a sense of injustice. It's hard to understand why so many clear-cut penalties were not awarded to the Reds in the first months of 2006/07, unless it's the referee's fear that any penalty for such a high-profile club instantly becomes a high-profile talking point.

Crossroads

It was perhaps no great revelation, but it has become increasingly clear that 2004 was a real crossroads for the club. A new manager, and new coaching personnel; a seriously revised playing staff (which has been largely regenerated in the past 30 months); the ongoing application for a new stadium, which in terms of the club's identity and infrastructure would represent the biggest change in its history; and the search for some kind of suitable investment, to help hold all of these plans — from purchasing the best players to constructing a state-of-the-art stadium — together in a way that safeguards the future. Jeopardising the future of Liverpool FC is one thing that cannot be gambled with; you need to speculate to accumulate, and that business maxim holds true in football. But the success of any team is nearly always related to its off-field strength, and in a classic chicken and egg situation, it's hard to say which comes first. Money buys better players; better players help win trophies and secure higher league placings and European football; and these combine to make more money. It's the same with a stadium. Success on the pitch puts bums on seats; bums on seats means more money; more money leads to the chance to build a bigger stadium, to get more bums on seats and make even more money. It also helps satisfy fan demand, and you get a new generation of paying customers who were otherwise unable to gain regular access to Anfield. But if the team does badly, demand for tickets drops.

What no-one wants is 40,000 people in the new stadium, with a hike in prices, but which still represents a massive shortfall for the club in terms of what it needs to be making to meet what will be fairly steep financial repayments. There will be a point in the future, 20-30 years down the line, when the 'mortgage' is paid off. But it's no point being homeless at that stage. Nor is it desirable to have a great home, but without the suitable furnishings: in 2025 we want to be watching the equivalent of Xabi Alonso, not the next Robbie Savage. It's not about Liverpool becoming the richest club, as even a packed 80,000-seater wouldn't ensure that. But it's about making the club competitive, and staying in touch with its rivals. Perhaps most importantly, it's about making the club appealing to future generations of top players. Anfield remains a legendary stadium, but it is also ageing and land-locked. The only acceptable solution, when it came to moving, was to relocate 300 yards, to Stanley Park, where the aura of Anfield could still be felt in the air. As with Wembley, something remains sacred about the name and the area.

In some ways, only now is the club close to exiting the 2004 crossroads, having first been stalled at one set of lights, while awaiting the green light on the next. On the pitch much has changed, and nearly all for the better. But behind the scenes there remains a delicate balancing act that awaits further attention. With the new stadium going ahead, the main issue in need of resolving is that of investment.

Comeback Kings

One of the distinctions I made between Gérard Houllier and Rafael Benítez was the latter's ability to get his team back into games in which they looked dead and buried. In that first season, the Spaniard managed three remarkable recoveries: away at Fulham, at home to Olympiakos and, lest we forget, the Champions League final itself. There was also a comeback from a Nicolas Anelka goal to win 2-1 in his first home league game, against Manchester City.

Clearly it was a valid trend. In his second season, Benítez managed two further remarkable turnarounds: from 3-1 down at Luton, to win 5-3, and in the FA Cup Final, when a 2-0 deficit to West Ham was overturned thanks to penalties. And then, in his third season, there was the August comeback against the Hammers, again in the first home game of the season.

Compared with Houllier's failure to have his team overturn a deficit between 1999 and 2004, it's a remarkable improvement. However, in Houllier's defence, he did also bring the Reds back from 3-0 down to draw with Basle; but whereas two of Benítez's most famous comebacks also ended in 3-3 draws, those games had penalties to decide the game.

The Curse of the No. 9 Shirt

Djibril Cissé's time in the no.9 shirt was not as disastrous as some might suggest, but it's fair to say that he didn't live up to expectations. Two horrific compound fractures during his time at the club — the second when representing France just ahead of the summer's World Cup — would be pretty indicative of some kind of serious curse.

Cissé's departure opened the way for Fowler to reclaim the no.9 for his back, after six months wearing 11, but he might have been better asking Jamie Carragher to give up 23 — the number in which the Toxteth striker had his best seasons. Fowler's Liverpool career originally ran aground with the famous centre-forward's numeral; two months into 2005/06, Fowler found himself unable to even make the match-day squad, be it the 16 for Premiership matches or the 18 for Europe. When he was then due to be called upon, a back injury sidelined him for a number of weeks.

While Fowler will never again be the carefree player who lit up the

Premiership a decade ago, it's also true that he cannot be written off. Upon his return the side, as captain against Reading in the Carling Cup, he scored a sublime goal with the outside of his left foot — one which definitely rolled back the years.

The comparisons with Anelka and Diouf, in looking at the players to have worn the number nine shirt in recent times, have become more interesting, with the former joining the latter at Bolton. Diouf had a fine season on loan at Bolton in 2004/05, but his second year at the Reebok, once he'd joined on a permanent deal, was a big letdown. His third season, however, seems to have found him back to his best. And, of course, back to his most irritating.

Anelka continues his nomadic existence, racking up yet more expensive transfer fees. Since leaving Arsenal for £23m, he's joined Paris St Germain for £20m, quickly followed by a return to the Premiership, and Manchester City, for £12m. His next destination was Fenerbahçe, for £7m, but it could so easily have been Liverpool; Benítez was toying with the idea of a move for the Frenchman, but instead opted for Fernando Morientes.

How different would things have been with a striker who was perfect for the Premiership, as opposed to the one who duly arrived and struggled? It seems pretty easy to conclude that Anelka would have performed better as an individual. But that's the thing with Anelka: while he is a team player in terms of his use of the ball, particularly outside the box, his mentality marks him down as someone who likes to go it alone. With Morientes in the team in 2005/06, Liverpool averaged 2.5 points per game, more than any other Red. Somehow he seemed to help gel things together, albeit in an unspectacular fashion. He was also a great team player, and certainly never upset the apple cart, in the way Anelka's reputation (and the influence of his brothers) suggests he could have.

The Frenchman, nicknamed 'Le Sulk', joined Bolton in 2006, for £8.2m, to take his total fees to more than £70m in seven years. Certainly no team has had the value for money that Arsenal found: £500,000 for a 17-year-old who would start 73 games and score 28 goals, including those that secured the Gunners the double in his debut season; followed by a £23m parting gift, courtesy of Real Madrid. Manchester City also got pretty good value for their £12m, with 38 goals in 89 games; recouping £5m less three years later, but at least he'd delivered consistently on the pitch. Fenerbahçe got a decent goals return — 14 in 39 games — and a league title to boot; to add to Anelka's double with Arsenal, and his European Cup with Madrid. If players can be judged on their medals collection alone (which, of course, they can't), he easily outstrips Alan Shearer.

Anelka's subsequent career, ever since Houllier said non, has been its usual mix of highs and lows, but he has showed enduring quality. It remains an interesting "what could have been" to ponder. The antics of Diouf make it hard to regret him ever leaving; the £10m fee and two inconsistent years leave you only regretting that he ever arrived in the first place.

But it seems that the Reds have finally solved the search for a top-class bought-in centre-forward. Following the record (or near-record) fees paid for Stan Collymore, Emile Heskey, Diouf and Cissé, all of whom failed to deliver on a consistent basis, the Reds have snaffled Dutchman Dirk Kuyt, a striker capable of plundering a sufficient amount of goals while displaying the necessary work ethic. But it doesn't end there. Craig Bellamy has the potential to be a real success, while Peter Crouch, with over 30 goals for club and country in the 12 months between December 2005 and 2006, is starting to find the net on a regular basis.

And then of course there's the current incumbent of the famous no.9 shirt: Robbie Fowler. How long can he hold onto it for?

Chelsea and expensive strikers

I find it interesting that I mentioned that Chelsea might not have been any better served with a world-class finisher like Andriy Shevchenko rather than a robust target-man like Didier Drogba. Now, some 18 months later, Mourinho has both players on board. At the time of writing, it is Drogba with all the goals. Shevchenko, the Rolls Royce, has thus far proved less effective than Drogba, the big Sherman Tank. Of course, that could all quickly change, as the former seeks to settle into a new style of play. But it also backs up the assertion that you can't just throw the best players in the world into a new team — even one so dominant — and expect them to flourish.

Djibril Cissé was more prolific in French football than Drogba, as I pointed out when comparing the two players after their first season in England. And in Cissé's one fully-fit season at Liverpool he outscored Drogba again (in all competitions at least), and this despite Benítez rotating him and deploying him on the right. Cissé's scoring rate in his minutes as a striker placed him 16th in the Premiership; Drogba's put him at 10th, having been 2nd the year before. So Drogba, for all his detractors, and for all his 'iffy' moments, has been a clear success. He has suited Chelsea's tactics perfectly on the way to back-to-back league titles, and that's the value of a manager buying a specific player to perform a particular role. The Ivory Coast striker's brute strength, allied to a real turn of pace and the occasional surprising piece of skill, marks him out as perfect for the English game.

Home Improvements

It's interesting to note that, with the exception of John Arne Riise and Steve Finnan, the players listed in this section of *Golden Past, Red Future* — relating to those who made the biggest leaps in progress — have all since been sold on. Igor Biscan, Milan Baros and Djimi Traoré all seemed to improve during Benítez's inaugural season, but none did enough to fully convince the Spaniard.

It shows that, for a perfectionist like Benítez, good is not good enough. Rarely has he bought a player who has proven a retrograde step on the man being replaced. Reina, in his initial season at least, was an improvement on Dudek, and at just 23, has plenty of time to establish himself. Sissoko quickly proved far more effective than even a resurgent Biscan, and was such a revelation that Didi Hamann was allowed to leave. While a player of Hamann's experience and calibre would always be very useful, he had dropped down the pecking order, and even more so when Benítez began to move towards a four-man midfield; even Steven Gerrard couldn't get many games in the centre. Hamann could not be kept happy as a squad member, and that was why he was allowed to leave.

Jan Kromkamp was better than Josemi (even if it was a short-lived experiment). Peter Crouch proved more prolific, and more creative, than Milan Baros. Dirk Kuyt instantly showed more gumption than Fernando Morientes. And Alonso was a big step up from Danny Murphy. With the exception of Michael Owen, who chose to leave, no one deemed expendable has been missed.

Fernando Morientes: it just never happened

My proclamations that Fernando Morientes would almost certainly come good in his second season were not without foundation; it seemed only a matter of time before such a class act sprang into life. I don't think I was alone in feeling he would be a great signing, although Guillem Balague, who, as a *La Liga* pundit, obviously knew his compatriot better, felt he'd not take easily to English football.

Niggling injuries never helped Morientes settle at Liverpool. He missed eight games early on in 2005/06, when it looked like he'd get a good run at the start of his first full season, and had another couple of spells on the sidelines. Whenever he had he good game, injury seemed to follow quickly on its heels (otherwise known as Smicer Syndrome). Goals came in dribs and drabs, but he never went on a run. At no point did he look like he'd totally licked English football; his body language was rarely right.

Such was the damage to his confidence he didn't even look any better in the Champions League: a competition in which he had rarely failed in the past, and which clearly suited his style of play. It showed the mental aspects behind his struggles. Arguably the club's most natural attacking header of a ball since John Toshack, he often met crosses more like John Inman. (For those of you unfamiliar with the innuendo-based 1970s British sitcom, Are You Being Served?, Inman's character was a bit like Mrs Slocombe's pussy.)

The comparison made with paying £6m either for Morientes or James Beattie (as did Everton) also remains interesting: up to now neither signing has proved a success. While Everton still have time to get their money's worth for their bulky striker, whose goals to date have come mostly from the penalty spot, Benítez called off his dalliance with his purchase from Real Madrid after 18 months. In that time, neither striker offered the kind of play the respective fans expected.

Yet for just a fraction more money, the much-derided Peter Crouch has proven both more effective and, surprisingly, more prolific than either. And in his early days at Goodison, Andy Johnson is belying his erstwhile reputation as a Birmingham City reject, and a man of distinctly First Division quality. (He finally got some revenge on Liverpool in the first Mersey derby of 2006/07, when his two goals will have helped erase the memory of his penalty miss in the 2001 Worthington Cup Final: the decisive moment when 'new' Liverpool started to come of age, on the way to that historic treble.)

When *Golden Past, Red Future* was commenced, Crouch was regarded as an utter failure in top-flight football, and was still a reserve at struggling Southampton. The peaks and troughs of some footballer's careers can be quite remarkable, and a lesson for life in how good can turn bad, and bad can turn good, in such a short space of time. Morientes joins Juan Sebastian Veron as living proof that there are no sure-fire hits, and that sometimes good footballers fail when the circumstances are not in their favour.

'El Moro' showed moments of class, with his goal at Charlton appearing the start of great things. But great things never materialised. He did have a positive effect on the team in certain ways, with his guile and experience helping link play and keep things tight ahead of the midfield, but too much appeared to be lacking.

A move to Valencia followed in the summer of 2006, as the trade route between the two clubs continued to flow (despite Benítez's acrimonious departure and subsequent successful legal battle). Upon his return Morientes quickly found his form and fitness — and indeed his feet — and plundered six goals in his first six games; half as many as he scored at Liverpool in 18 months.

Harry Kewell, Aussie Crock

Labelled an 'enduring enigma' in *Golden Past, Red Future* , that tag is still firmly attached to the player who should have been to this generation what John Barnes was to a previous one.

As predicted, Kewell did indeed come good in a Liverpool shirt in 2005/06, with Benítez playing the Aussie most weeks in the second half of the season, once his fitness had been proven. He scored three superb goals (still not enough, mind), and gave real balance to the side. Results improved once he was fit, and while it may be partly coincidental, anyone involved in a regular improvement of fortunes deserves his due credit. On his better days he left defenders for dead, as of old.

But then it all went wrong again, as another cup final loomed: yet again he regained enough fitness to be considered for a starting berth on the big occasion — having been the Reds' star man in the semi-final — but yet again he limped disconsolately from the action with the cup itself at stake. Similarly, he worked hard to be fit for the World Cup, and having missed the opening game produced a virtuoso display, and the crucial goal, in securing his country's passage to the last 16 for the first-ever time; but again it came at the price of injury, and Australia's biggest occasion would go ahead without its best player. A number of operations followed, and 2006/07 was in danger of being written-off before it ever began for the beleaguered winger. In late October he admitted it would be 2007 before he was fit again.

It's impossible to judge a half-fit player amongst and against fully fit peers. Such is the professionalism in football these days, in terms of fitness, pace and power, any weakness is quickly exposed. Some players can get by when carrying a knock, but few can do so when carrying a muscle injury. Bruising hurts, but the pain ebbs with adrenaline; it can be 'run off'. A damaged muscle, however, is a tear waiting to happen.

Can Kewell become the player many trust he could be? With every passing year it becomes harder to believe with any certainty. Some players are naturally prone to injury. There are those, like Michael Owen, whose problems recur partly down to the scar tissue in a damaged muscle, and partly because their style of running, combined with innate muscular-skeletal disorders, presents risks. Others get into a vicious cycle of new injuries, when the return from one leads to an imbalance in the body's make-up, and causes a new ailment. Kewell appears to be suffering from both recurrent problems (the groin, which has now been operated on) and new issues, too: the calf and the septic arthritis, with the latter initially misdiagnosed as gout, a condition usually associated with elderly alcoholics. The only positive from all these injuries is that while he's been laid up he's been 'saving' other parts of his body; the wear and tear to his knees will have been minimal in the past three seasons, compared to someone who's played 150 games in that time. But of course, there's no point Kewell having pristine knees if they are the only remotely healthy part of his crumbling body.

It's also true that wingers tend to do better in the earlier stages of their careers, when at their speediest and most daring, although the best can mature into other roles, as seen with John Barnes and Ryan Giggs. Kewell's ability as a second-striker has never been in doubt, and he could yet make some kind of impact there with his vision and game intelligence; in many ways it's his best position, and certainly the one in which Benítez first saw him perform, on a visit to England in 1999. It's still too early to write off such a natural talent, but talent without fitness just leaves a player who can beat a man with a trick but not manage to get away from him before the recovery tackle bites in. All players need to be as close to 100% fit as possible to stand any chance of succeeding in the modern game. But those who use their brains have an added advantage; the first two yards are in the mind, as the saying goes.

Pennant's pennance

In *Golden Past, Red Future* I was heavily critical of Jermaine Pennant, particularly an apparent lack of self-awareness after various problems at Arsenal. That made it interesting for me when he signed for the Reds in 2006. In fairness to the player, he had rebuilt his career somewhat in the interim. Liverpool can only hope, and trust, that, as appears to be the case, he has genuinely grown up since those early days. He was very young at the time, and had experienced a big-money move to the bright lights of London when only his mid-teens. But it was also a damning indictment of young English players in general, and how susceptible they can be to going off the rails given this country's attitude to alcohol, as well as an alarmingly inability for people to take responsibility for their own actions. The spotlight footballers are under merely highlights those shortcomings.

"I have no regrets about going to Arsenal as a 16 year-old," Pennant says. "But if I had the chance again I would have come to Liverpool when I was 16. I am just thrilled to be here now. There were bad times as well as good times for me at Arsenal, but overall I enjoyed my years there. That was one of the choices I made in life and I had to live with it but I am at Liverpool now so I couldn't have done too much wrong." I'd argue that he actually did a fair amount wrong — nothing to make him one of Britain's Ten Most Wanted (criminals, not players), but more than enough that can be considered wrong for a *professional* footballer. But by getting his head down at Birmingham, following a spell in jail and having to play with an electronic tracking device, he has earned his second chance. However, he's now old enough to have few excuses if he slips from the straight and narrow.

Jamie Carragher was no tearaway, but he needed pulling into line by Gérard Houllier; Liverpool are now reaping the benefits of a young man steered onto the right path at the right time. But Carragher also had the character to succeed. Ashley Cole, the one Englishman to come through the ranks at Arsenal (the rest simply never proved good enough) at a time when Pennant felt his chances were harmed by his nationality, showed his loyalty by agitating for a move to Chelsea. Cole claimed he nearly crashed his car when he heard the club were not going to offer him £60,000 a week, but a mere £55,000. Poor soul. It's not just foreigners who lack loyalty.

Pennant also bucks a trend that was identified in *GPRF*: that of the big four clubs never releasing a young player who was good enough to later find himself back at one of the elite sides. It's a slightly different situation, in that Pennant wasn't allowed to leave Highbury because of a lack of ability; it was more down to problems off the field, and the quality Arsenal had in the position in which he played. Pennant hadn't radically failed to reach his rich potential, which had made him a £2m 15-year-old; he was falling short, bit not disastrously and irreversibly so. It was clear he was still a Premiership player, with a future in the game — if he woke up to himself, and his shortcomings. That seems to be the case, on the early evidence of his time at Anfield, but it's how he overcomes any setbacks or spells on the sidelines that will prove whether or not he's matured.

Jeepers Keepers

During 2004/05 there were clearly a number of concerns surrounding the goalkeepers on the Reds' books. Jerzy Dudek, so capable of brilliance during the campaign, was also a nervous wreck at times. Chris Kirkland was more of a physical wreck. And Scott Carson was a mere rookie. Between them they made 17 errors that led to Liverpool conceding goals.

At the time of finishing *Golden Past, Red Future*, a move for Pepe Reina was being mooted. But it still seemed as if Chris Kirkland, if he could get fit, would stand a chance of making the spot his own. Clearly that was not the case. Benítez had a different type of keeper in mind: a quicker, sharper type of custodian who could also sweep up behind the back four, and thus allow the defence the chance to position themselves further up the field.

Was the uncertain goalkeeping situation solved with the arrival of Reina? Well, in his first season, that certainly appeared the case. But then Jerzy Dudek had a storming first year at Anfield, and swiftly unravelled. All players have intermittent confidence crises, but goalkeepers, as the most exposed player in the team, are more vulnerable. They are a breed unto themselves.

It's been an interesting ride for Reina. Early in his Liverpool career he looked decidedly shaky. He had an absolute nightmare at Birmingham in the league. But he then found some real consistency, and from that point until the spring only really erred at Bolton. Then came some criticism in the FA Cup semi-final against Chelsea, although he was forced into emergency action when attempting to punch John Arne Riise's poor header. He clearly messed up for the second goal in the final itself, fumbling an easy shot into the path of Dean Ashton. The third goal, courtesy of Paul Konchesky's over-hit cross, was also debited as a Reina error, but was pretty unsavable. Keepers cannot be psychic and position themselves for an unusual delivery; if Reina had been protecting his back post then he'd have left the rest of the goal gaping.

But it was at the start of his second season when criticism of the Spaniard grew fairly intense. With high-profile errors at the end of 2005/06 still fresh in the mind, he allowed a mis-hit Bobby Zamora cross to beat him at his near post, as playing West Ham again gave him nightmares. While his positioning was spot-on, the sheer unpredictable and unreadable nature of the fluke caught him off guard; he got both hands to the ball, but having done so his wrists were too 'soft'. There's a unwritten rule that goalkeepers should not be beaten at their near post, but not everything is easy to deal with. Much more galling was how Reina palmed an Everton shot into the air at Goodison Park; compounding the error by fluffing an attempt to gather the second ball, and in so doing, presenting Andy Johnson with a simple finish. In some ways it was Reina's pro-active mindset that caused this dire mistake. With the game in injury time, and the Reds two goals down, he was trying to avoid conceding a corner, which was the easy option; he wanted to keep hold of the ball, to start a move, as is his wont. His momentum took him over his own goalline, and as he released the ball he allowed the Everton striker to poach. It was the last kind of goal you want to concede in a Mersey derby, and a thoroughly depressing moment in the season.

Interestingly, very few of his errors in the past year have actually cost the Reds points or lost them games. The FA Cup semi-final was won 2-1, and the final won on penalties — thanks to the keeper's brilliance. (Indeed, in a mirroring of Dudek's Istanbul heroics, his remarkable save in the last minute of injury time took the game to spot kicks, where his sharp reflexes won the day.) The Zamora goal in the league game in August was overturned by two second-half strikes, and the Everton game was 99.9% over when he messed up.

All players make mistakes. A central midfielder will often miscontrol the ball. Obviously there is more control in the hands than in the feet, so keepers should not be fumbling easy catches, as did Reina at Cardiff. But there's also an hysteria that surrounds goalkeeping errors. Since he arrived at Liverpool, Reina has made a relatively low number of goal-costing mistakes.

As 2007 approaches, the Reds have three first choice Premiership goalkeepers: as well as Reina, Kirkland has been custodian at Wigan, and Scott Carson was receiving a baptism of fire at Charlton, who spent the early part of the season rooted to the foot of the table. Both loaned keepers were winning rave reviews, but it's a very different game for them at club where clean sheets aren't demanded and where they're kept busy. At Liverpool it's about concentration and being able to handle the pressure, and as previously mentioned, about sweeping behind the defence with the current manager.

Revisiting Alan Hansen's Criticism

The book's criticisms of Alan Hansen's analysis of Benítez's spending policy (made by the ex-captain in the Telegraph in January 2005) still stand. Time has done nothing to alter the conclusions drawn almost two years ago. The Scot's comments — that Benítez was wrong to look to Spain for his signings — never made much sense at the time, and still don't; however, everyone is entitled to an aberration now and again, and perhaps even Hansen himself has changed his mind, as is his right. But it just didn't fit with logic that Benítez should focus on the English market, either then or now. Gérard Houllier's poor purchases from France were in no way linked to Benítez's buys from Spain; yet Hansen managed to do so. While only an opinion piece, Hansen was guilty of making concrete assessments at a difficult time for Benítez; assessments that, rather than buy him some time by offering an understanding of the problems the manager faced, only served to intensify the criticism.

Benítez has continued to successfully mine Spanish football for some of its finer talents; on the whole his record of buys from *La Liga* still appears outstanding [*and appears even better after 2007*], while he's picked up some gems in other European leagues, too. To get even 50% of purchases spot-on, from any market, is an achievement. Value-for-money has been found with the vast majority of all inward transfers; but it's not been a case of buying cheap players who have looked okay for the outlay — Xabi Alonso, Luis Garcia, Momo Sissoko and Pepe Reina have all contributed to the significant improvements and the additional silverware now in the trophy cabinet. Each has proved an inspired signing, although time will be the judge of their ultimate success.

Mark Gonzalez looks an exciting acquisition. It's too early to say whether or not he's the real deal, as he adapts to the English game, but his record in Spain, and flashes of quality in a red shirt, suggest he will prove a success in the long-term. His goal within three minutes of his debut proved to be the decisive strike in qualifying for the Champions League group stages, and he scored the all-important first goal against Spurs in his first Premiership start.

Josemi, Pellegrino and Nunez came and went pretty quickly. Each offered something during their brief stay, whether it be numbers in the squad to rest more senior players (especially in the case of Pellegrino for Hyypia), or the occasional important contribution, but none can be considered anything approaching a success. Kromkamp, who came in a swap deal from Villarreal, looked an upgrade on Josemi, but even the Dutchman was dispensed with within six months. Nunez, Josemi and Kromkamp all recouped money when sold.

Morientes was the exception, as the one moderately-expensive player with a big reputation who arrived at a good age and simply failed to deliver. It wasn't that he was terrible, more that he was average.

It's not just Benítez who has continued to look overseas for the best talent. Chelsea still look to the continent, as do Arsenal, last year's beaten Champions League finalists. Of the 'big four', only Manchester United have a more insular outlook, and their attitude comes at a hefty premium. Ultimately, it has to be about getting the right players, irrespective of their nationality or their current playing location. If they are what the team needs, and the price is not prohibitive, then a deal must be sought. The player's own abilities and attitude are what counts; not his passport. (Although, of course, passports can provide their own side issues.)

Buying players from the Premiership has always been couched with its own problems. It's interesting that Peter Crouch and Craig Bellamy both struggled in front of goal initially, when neither had the league or language to adapt to. Crouch eventually proved a very effective signing, but it's also true that it was a rather left-field purchase; perhaps the genius of it was that no other big club sought to make a move for a player who was coming into his own, and who offered a style of play that even the best defenders could be foxed by, even if he wasn't going to challenge Zinedine Zidane in the grace stakes. Any other current England international striker would have cost far more money, although Crouch's appeal was not his price tag but his unique playing style, and the particular kind of problems he poses defenders. In *Golden Past, Red Future* I made the statement about teams always looking to utilise the long ball to freakishly tall players, and that comes from making assumptions about players based on brief glimpses; Crouch had always been noted for having a good touch for a big man, but that's also always been a backhanded compliment in the football lexicon. Watching Crouch closely, you get to see he has a good touch irrespective of his height, and I happily stand corrected on the extent of that.

It can be a challenge to settle at a new club, and in a new environment, whatever your nationality. Jermaine Pennant was another who had some difficulty when arriving at Anfield — in stark contrast to Dirk Kuyt, who was hugely impressive in all his early games. (Then again, the Dutch do tend to speak better English than a lot of Brits, so that's one less barrier. And Kuyt's style is more Anglo-Saxon than any recent English striker bar Alan Shearer. The perm, however, is distinctly Dutch porn star.) [*While Pennant generally improved, Kuyt started to struggle in his second season.*]

Money remains the big obstacle in purchasing from England. The signing of Bellamy was only made possible by the release clause in his contract; otherwise he'd have been too costly. To put the English market into perspective, Benítez managed to buy both Alonso and Sissoko for £2m less than Alex Ferguson paid for Michael Carrick. Daniel Agger was relatively expensive at £5.8m, but that's still less than a fifth of what Rio Ferdinand cost Manchester United in 2002. Kuyt cost around £10m, but had he been at another English club that his price tag would have been double that.

The fees Benítez has paid for British talent have tended to be around the £6-7m mark (similar to the kind of prices he paid for overseas players), and as such pretty reasonable given the market. He has also picked up promising youngsters for less than £1m; Scott Carson and Paul Anderson seem certain to be valued at least five times as highly in years to come. [*Carson's current value, as of January 2008, is over ten times what Liverpool paid.*]

So it's reasonable to conclude that Benítez has used the funds at his disposal to good effect, no matter what the market. He has had a strong sense of what he has been after in a player, and on the whole has found what he was looking for. It just takes time for some of the cheaper, younger players to mature.

Alan Hansen: Hitting the Wrong Targets Again

Almost two years after I pulled apart an Alan Hansen attack on low-flying Liverpool, which I've just discussed, the ex-captain was back with some more heavy criticisms. I've no problem with him criticising the club, and if there was ever a time to be critical of performances it was late October 2006, after the disappointing reversal at Manchester United. But I just wish he'd show a bit more balance in his approach to criticism. For me, he was as off-target as many of the Reds' shots that left them in the bottom half of the table.

There were problems at the time of his criticisms. And the performance at Old Trafford, once United scored, was incredibly limp, as the confidence visibly drained from the players. But too many of the things Hansen identified in his *Telegraph* column were lazy criticisms dressed up as facts.

United's success in the game came through three home-grown players immersed in the club, according to Hansen. But Liverpool had two of their own out there, Gerrard and Carragher, and neither played well. Gerrard seemed to too frustrated with events to lead the team, while Carragher, despite his unstinting effort, was at fault in some way for both goals (the second due to injury, admittedly).

Why did Hansen hash up all the talk of locals again, when there were so few during Hansen's halcyon days? Why are they suddenly integral to success? Xabi Alonso, a Spaniard, gives 100% every single game, even if he's not a blood-and-thunder type player. He *cares*. His form had been stodgy in the early part of 2006/07, but Benítez had just had two great years from him. The same can be said of Carragher and Gerrard. All three care; but none was playing anywhere near their best.

Momo Sissoko, who'd only been at the club 15 months, was the Reds' best player at Old Trafford, all over the pitch working his extra-long socks off. He's not local, nor immersed in the club. He's just a great player and a hard worker with lungs of titanium. Sami Hyypia's commitment could never be questioned, even if his form at times can be. How local is he?

As for Hansen's talk of the Reds lacking a striker capable of 20 league goals a season since the sale of Michael Owen, it has to be pointed out that Owen never actually scored 20 league goals in a season. Of course, he came close, with a 19 and a couple of 18s, and was capable of getting 20 if he ever stayed fit long enough (which, of course, he never could). But where did that get the Reds? Not as many points as Benítez's team managed last season, with no striker even making double figures, while the top scoring striker on the run to winning the European Cup in 2005 was Milan Baros, with just two goals. Chelsea have won the league the last two years with low-scoring forwards, as have teams on a number of occasions since the Premiership began. While a 20-goal-a-season striker is an obvious bonus (providing he's not a liability in other areas), it's a myth that one is essential.

Dirk Kuyt could well be capable of 20 Premiership goals a season, and that has to be the aim, but he needs time to adjust. By the start of November he'd scored more than twice as many league goals as £30m Shevchenko, rated the best finisher in the world, in far less minutes on the pitch. It took Michael Owen, whom Hansen rightly uses as an example of a reliably finisher, a while to adapt to life in Madrid, and to find his scoring boots. So why should Kuyt be any different here? Newcastle have since paid £17m for Owen, and will be lucky to get more than ten games out of him in his first two seasons. While I'd have liked to have seen Owen back at Anfield, he'd have been little use on crutches. The four strikers Benítez had at his disposal — Kuyt, Bellamy,

Crouch and Fowler — were all capable of scoring at a good rate, and sharing 30-40 league goals between them. *[They finished with 29.]*

Hansen then said the club's limited funds mean it has to buy 'maybe' players who cost between £4-9m: "That gets you 'maybe' players, footballers who could do a job but who would be dangerous to rely on in a crisis."

Judging players *purely* by their transfer value is crazy. While more money gives you more choice, and more chance to outbid anyone to get who you really want, it doesn't mean you'll *definitely* get a better player. If you pick up great players near the end of their current deals, or with clauses in their contracts, you can do business more cleverly. Paying £4-9m increases your chances of getting 'maybe' players, clearly, but it does not mean that is all you can possibly get, particularly if you take your time, shop around and thoroughly scout targets.

There are plenty of examples of great players who broke transfer records and were undoubted successes; but there are also plenty of examples of cheap players whose reputations grew massively once they signed for a big club. The same is true in reverse: mega-deals have resulted in mega-flops, and sometimes if you pay peanuts you really do get monkeys.

Pepe Reina was in that low-to-medium price range, and he was superb in his first season, as he had been in Spain for a number of years, despite still being just 23; but then, as a young keeper, he found himself struggling at the start of his second season; did that mean he needs to be written off? Momo Sissoko was another. He's been a real steal, and while he can be rash with his passing he's already a superb player at such a tender age, and possibly a £20m midfielder in the making. Daniel Agger cost a fraction under £6m, and was voted PFA Player of the Month for September, after a quite exceptional start to the season by the young Dane. He is an absolute gem.

Finnan, Riise and Hyypia all cost £4m or less. The new players, like Gonzalez and Pennant, cost in Hansen's quoted bracket. But like all new players they needed time to settle; Shevchenko cost £30m and at the time of Hansen's piece had yet to impress. You cannot even start to write off any new players before at least six months at a new club, and up to a year if in a new country. Too many top class talents have taken that long, or even longer, to adapt. *[Gonzalez did indeed prove a 'maybe' player, which proves Hansen's point to a degree, but then I'm not arguing that you can end up with failures; just that you can also end up with great purchases.]*

As for the point on big spending, when Liverpool have shelled out in excess of £10m over the years, only Xabi Alonso has so far been worth the money. (Kuyt, who cost between £9-10m, should prove good value, too.) But Diouf? Heskey? Cissé? They turned out to be 'maybe' players. *If that.*

As with Hansen's criticisms two years ago, his assertion that spending little has resulted in average players made no sense based on what the Reds had actually procured for such fees over recent seasons. There's also the fact that Benítez has had 80% of the squad to rebuild since 2004, rather than merely needing to add a couple of players; so the money had to be spread fairly evenly across a number of purchases. The option of more money always helps, of course, as it gives more possibilities and acts as an insurance on bad buys (you can always, with impunity, go straight out and buy someone else). But there's no simple solution to finding such riches.

There were also serious problems with the back four, according to Hansen. But it was much the same personnel as 2005/06, when it was the best around; could it be that was down to form and confidence? After all, they proved how good they could be on the way to 33 clean sheets, even when the full-backs were heavily rotated. They hadn't all become bad players overnight, had they? *[And by the end of 2006/07, Pepe Reina had yet again won the Golden Gloves for most Premiership clean sheets, while the defence helped the Reds make it to Athens.]*

While I agree with Hansen's assertions that the centre of defence is not an area to *needlessly* tinker with, Sami Hyypia was struggling for form at the point when Daniel Agger came in, with Carragher injured. Agger played so well it meant one defender had to drop out when Carragher was fit, so it was only going to be Hyypia. Except when it came to playing at Bolton in late September, where the aerial bombardment was on the cards, so a switch to the Finn was made.

Then Agger, the best defender in the league at the time, broke his hand with Denmark. So it was not so much rotation as enforced changes — plus one understandable tactical change (especially after a couple of headers had just been conceded against Galatasaray). Manchester United had rotated their team as heavily as Liverpool in the league when the two teams met, but it was working for them. Then again, it worked for the Reds in 2005/06. Doesn't that suggest that blaming rotation is a cop out?

Hansen says the Reds did not look capable of going on a run like the one at the end of last season, but a year earlier the same could have been said; and the Reds went on two outstanding runs, not just the one Hansen mentioned, having also had a similar slump between January and March.

Was Benítez making mistakes? Almost certainly. But hindsight is a wonderful thing. All managers can be said to have made mistakes if their team has lost. Were the players also making mistakes? Of course. Low confidence does that; but confidence cannot be restored with a pep talk. If it could, there'd never be any shortage of confidence in the sport, or indeed any other sport. The problem at Liverpool, to my mind, was that too many players, including nearly all of the key men, were low on confidence following dips in their own form, and once it affects the team as a whole it gets that much harder to do anything about it. You can't 'rest' an entire team.

So while I maintain that Alan Hansen has every right to air his views, and to be critical where appropriate, I'd like to see him take a little more time in thinking about what he's saying and to use that great knowledge of his in a more astute manner. He needs to stop talking in black and whites, as football is rarely that simple. I don't have it in for the Reds' legend — far from it — but I do expect better from him. As with the kind of criticisms made by the Liverpool board member in late October 2006, Hansen's opinion, as an ex-captain, carries a lot of weight. It gets noticed. And the public start to buy into it. People still thought Liverpool were terrible at defending set-pieces in 2005/06, despite having the best record in the league, because the myth gets continuously recycled. It's the same with rotation: both Chelsea and Manchester United, who sat 1st and 2nd in the table at the time Benítez was castigated for doing so, had rotated heavily. Liverpool had made just one more personnel change in games up to October 28th than Manchester United, who were the 2nd-most rotated team in the Premiership. Chelsea were the 3rd-most rotated.

Too many people believe what they are told, without actually looking at the underlying facts.

Alas, that's something that may never change.

Half-term report:
Not bad, but need to do better

January 2008

It says a lot about expectations at Liverpool, and the requirements for the remainder of the season, that two wins and two draws over the holiday period, from two home games and two away, is seen as some kind of disaster. I remember when averaging two points a game was what you aimed for.

And now there's more talk of Benítez being a "dead man walking". The atmosphere, and the pressure, surrounding the club is starting to make it seem impossible to succeed, with its undermining influence — unless some kind of siege mentality can be summoned. Any poor result has the spectre of a larger failure looming, and that's only going to prove detrimental.

Jurgen Klinsmann — a great player — is again being liked with Rafa's job, but what has he done as a coach/manager? Really, it baffles me to see him linked with top jobs.

I thought top clubs had moved away from appointing figurehead players as managers? Klinsmann took Germany to the semi-finals of the World Cup. But he did so on German soil, with the fans behind the team. Even England make the semi-finals of tournaments held in this country; South Korea did the same on home soil. How does a career of managing half a dozen competitive games (as Germany were automatically at the Finals) qualify Klinsmann for a job like managing Liverpool?

What is he like at buying players? What are his tactics? How does he man-manage? Does he stick around long, especially when the going gets tough? There is a gulf of difference between Benítez's proven knowledge and ability and some rookie who's done virtually nothing in the job, and never managed a club. He could be great, and he certainly has charisma, but where's the evidence he can manage a top club? I know this is only paper talk, but if there is even a fraction of truth in it, I'll despair. *[It turns out there was some truth in it, dating back to November 2007: Tom Hicks admitted in January 2008 that the German represented their contingency plan should Benítez leave.]*

There's a lot of doom and gloom around, and it's understandable; another year without a title challenge — or so it seems. I think the Reds can get back in amongst the title race with a few wins on the spin, but not to the point where a real challenge can be made; there's just no margin for error, and hasn't been for a few weeks now.

All of the top teams had bad games over Christmas, but United sneaked one more point from their four matches, despite a deserved defeat at West Ham and a poor home performance against Birmingham. And Chelsea got the kind of luck, with Kalou's offside goal, that Liverpool were not blessed with.

The Reds deserved to win all four games based on possession and clear-cut chances, although the Derby and Wigan displays were clearly substandard. The Reds could have used more luck, but also more inspiration. Having been leading, the Wigan game felt more like a defeat.

These days, drawing against teams like Wigan and Birmingham is as bad as it gets at Anfield; it's not great, obviously, but prior to Benítez arriving, the Reds lost home games to Bradford, Watford, Charlton, Manchester City, Southampton and Leicester, and to some of those teams on more than one occasion. I'm not suggesting that by not being as bad as that, the Reds are therefore 'great', but it's worth remembering those true low points all the same. These days, only the top sides come away with all three points.

Benítez's team performed much, much better away at Man City, in the most one-sided 0-0 draw in history. I think it was the first time I've ever seen a supposed top side defend like that at home: acting like they were a Conference side with the bus parked in front of the goal, but still offering some kind of implied threat, with a lot of pace to hit on the counter.

I wrote a lot about Rafa's tactics and methods in *Above Us Only Sky*, and nothing has really changed my opinion: while Arsenal, Chelsea and United may do things differently, there's nothing inherently wrong with how Rafa works based on the examples I discussed. Two years ago Ferguson had "lost the plot", and Wenger has also had a lot of criticism for not altering his thinking on certain issues, but once a team starts winning again, it all gets forgotten. (Maybe psychology and motivation are areas where the Reds could improve.)

Things are steadily improving under Benítez, and so many things are better than before he arrived (such as not only qualifying for the Champions League every single season, but also making the knockout stages, and, unbelievably, two finals in three seasons), but other teams are improving too, and the Premiership title is becoming an obsession. Then again, some other teams who've spent big, like Spurs and Newcastle, are really in the mire.

The Reds' home form has been the main problem, but in the previous three seasons it was excellent. The introduction of pace up front has helped the team away from home, but maybe the balance has gone a little awry at Anfield. But that can all change: the personnel is there for the team to be better at home than it has been. Maybe it just needs a little more understanding between the players, and a bit more luck and/or ruthlessness in front of goal.

But it's been a season beset from the start by problems: a lot of new players to blend quickly into a cohesive team; the fallout with, and departure of, Pako Ayestaran, which could have been either man's fault (or a bit of both); lack of centre-back cover after the belated ruling regarding Gabriel Heinze; the unprecedented public spat between manager and owners, and the increased pressure surrounding the club as a result; and while not quite an injury crisis, a fair few notable absentees: Agger, Alonso, Pennant, Torres, Aurelio and Kewell have all missed from a fair few games to a handful of months — although the latter two players aren't surprises on that score.

But all of those listed are technical players, and in the case of Agger, Benítez has been shorn of the one player who can step from defence into midfield and give a move impetus, as well as altering the dynamics of the play. His superb passing from the back is also sorely missed, as are his goals — he was starting to chip in with a fair few. For me he is easily the best footballing centre-back in the country, and while Hyypia has at least matched his defensive abilities, the creative side of Agger's game is irreplaceable.

Unlike in the previous seasons since the title last arrived, there's no-one at the club taking (or seriously on) the piss, or who hasn't had a lot of good games for the club (unlike *real* deadwood, like Diao, Cheyrou, et al). The mentality is mostly of winners, individually at least. But one thing you cannot buy, or create, is the assurance that comes once a team has landed its first league title.

There's still plenty of room for improvement from a number of players, but the nature of a big squad (which is needed) is that some players will flourish and others will stagnate. You can't give equal playing time to 25 players. And while Rafa continues to rotate, he sticks to a core of his best players.

Of those who have featured more than a couple of times, I'd exempt from blame: Torres, Reina, Gerrard, Carragher, Agger, Arbeloa, Alonso, Mascherano, Babel, Benayoun, Hyypia, Lucas, Hobbs and Finnan. That doesn't mean all are perfect, or were in form the whole time (Carragher, Gerrard and Finnan certainly had slow starts to the season).

But on the whole I cannot fault their contribution to the first half of the campaign (in some cases when age or settling into English football is taken into account), and see them all as important players for the future. Even Hyypia: after his excellent form deputising for Agger, it's clear he's up to another year or two in the squad.

Once he settled back into the team, the Finn, with 22 starts already, has largely been outstanding. I've always maintained he can play well into his late 30s, and while I started to get concerned that he might be ready to be put out to pasture early in the season, he has shown it to be merely rustiness. Another centre-back is needed, until Hobbs — who has immense potential — matures. He's a great 19-year-old centre-back, but it'll take a few years to be a great top-level centre-back.

Finding a partner for Fernando Torres — someone to play just behind him — seems to be the main concern. It's a role that Ryan Babel prefers, and in time one he may well make his own; he has the potential to just that. At the moment he lacks the necessary experience, and it's perhaps better that he adjusts to life in the Premiership on the wings, where there's more time and space. In the centre, there's often a crowd.

But another idea is Yossi Benayoun, a player who has always reminded me of Peter Beardsley in playing style and movement; he can create, score and also works hard. He started his career as a second-striker, and at the very least he seems an option worth considering.

I still believe that Benítez has constructed an excellent — and I mean excellent — young spine for this team. Reina, Agger, Carragher (the 'old man' of it), Mascherano, Alonso, Gerrard and Torres are all top, top players: gifted, committed, dedicated and born winners. That spine can only get better, and stronger. Lucas is surely another world-class central midfielder in the making, and Ryan Babel can add himself to the list of top spine players, if he matures to become the second-striker many feel is possible.

Were Benítez to be sacked, or walk away, as the press are yet again suggesting, the first concern would be how the Latin contingent would respond. They're professionals, and paid to get on with it, but it would clearly disappoint and, to some degree, disrupt players like Torres, Alonso and Reina. Then there's the question of how a new manager would alter things, and the process of learning new systems and introducing yet more new players.

While I am still 100% convinced that Rafa is the right man for the job, and is shaping something that he is best qualified to utilise, I do also think that any replacement, should things pan out that way, would inherit a quite superb nucleus of core players, and a lot of very promising youngsters. But as I write, Rafa is very much still in his job.

Aside from the issue of who to play just behind Torres, the problems lie mostly in the wider areas, as they have for a couple of years.

Finnan and Arbeloa are excellent full-backs; no real problem there. Although neither is outstanding going forward, both are good technical players who overlap when the wide midfielders tuck inside, and can play their part in fluid attacks. Elsewhere in wide areas there are a lot of decent to very-good players, and in Babel, one potentially great one, but none who are currently up there with the very best — in terms of consistency if nothing else.

Babel is not yet a totally effective winger, although he has the pace, skill and strength to mirror John Barnes at his best. He's still two years younger than Digger when he arrived, and unlike the former no.10, has to adapt to a new league at the same time. I really see such enormous potential in Babel, but at present he's struggling to pull his game together for more than a few minutes here and there, mostly when appearing as a sub — which, in the circumstances, is perfectly natural. He's on a steep learning curve.

Steven Gerrard is still the most effective and complete wide player the Reds have, and that's not necessarily a bad thing — in that at least the Reds *do have him*. In 2005/06 he was excellent out there, and scored a lot of goals; but he doesn't seem happy with the role.

To a degree I can understand why, but it's a shame — if he was really enthusiastic about it (rather than doing it as a chore), Benítez could have him marauding up and down that flank as well as cutting into the middle to score goals, with two from Alonso, Mascherano and Lucas holding the fort down in the middle and controlling the tempo of the game. That would make the Reds strong from left to right.

For me, a midfield four of Babel (or a fit, in-form Kewell, if such a thing can still exist), Alonso, Mascherano and Gerrard looks as strong as any around — on paper, at least. But as it stands, by putting Gerrard on the right the manager would have to gamble with a player who will do a job there, but whose heart clearly wouldn't be in it.

Rafa tried Gerrard behind Torres against Wigan, to get Alonso and Mascherano into the same side, but for some reason Gerrard can't adapt to the role quite as well as he should.

In theory it's a dream striking combination — the pair have 28 goals between them by the start of January — but the captain seems happiest coming onto the play from deeper areas, and seems unhappy with his back to goal. Maybe it's something that can be worked on; with his pace, power and eye for goal, he should be able to become a real force in the position. And as mentioned earlier, Babel has similar qualities, but will need time.

I'm not *entirely* sure why Crouch hasn't played more, but at the same time, I'm baffled why people keep asking me about an agenda against the player from Rafa. There's no suggestion of a falling out, and Rafa obviously rates him: he bought him, and played him a lot in the previous first two seasons, even when everyone called him insane for doing so. So for me, it's more a tactical concern.

Crouch is most effective as the main striker — the target man — as is Torres. Neither is at his best behind another striker. And no top team plays two out-and-out strikers pushed up the whole time. In fact, United's success this season has been without any main strikers: both Tevez and Rooney like to come deep, and neither has the physical attributes to be a target man.

Chelsea were better with just Drogba up front, before Shevchenko was shoe-horned in. Players who can operate in the hole, or between the lines, are essential. Crouch can do this, but it's not his strong suit. And Torres can certainly do this, but then you lose his pace against the last defender. So that's a problem.

In his first season, Kuyt really impressed me: a decent amount of goals (all the better considering he didn't take any penalties, and came close on a number of occasions, hitting the woodwork six times), a good amount of assists, as well as a quite stupendous work-rate. Against Barcelona and Chelsea in the Champions League he was really immense.

But this season, despite some sterling showings and signs of a promising partnership with Torres, his contribution in the final third has gradually wilted, to the point where it's almost non-existent. His lack of pace is hugely frustrating — an extra yard or two and he'd be right in the top bracket. He has a lot of game intelligence, both in and out of possession, but often gets closed off when he's about to shoot from a lack of that extra yard of pace.

But he's a battler, and a winner, and his work-rate does lift the other players. The more totally committed, never-say-die men in the squad, the better. And if he can rediscover his early season form, he looks a good foil for Torres.

Despite this, he currently looks like one of the players who, if a better alternative can be found, will slip down the pecking order. You can't improve on players like Torres and Gerrard, but you can on Kuyt, even if it's not easy to find the right man.

Momo Sissoko is another who started his Liverpool career brightly, and appeared to have a wonderful future, only for it to fall away.

Sissoko had two excellent seasons, although the second one trailed off towards the end. With the emergence of Lucas and the arrival of Mascherano, I would have no problem with the manager cashing in on the Malian if the price is anywhere near what has been quoted; unlike a lot of the other players some fans are disillusioned with, he could be considered surplus to requirements on account of the sheer quality he's competing with. But I still think he's an underrated player — one for whom people always focus on what he gets wrong.

It's really hard to know what to make of Harry Kewell these days. His footballing intelligence is always going to be there — he's a clever, consistent passer. But the other kind of passing — when it relates to overtaking a full-back — currently looks a thing of the past; at least on any kind of consistent basis. While apparently over his injuries, he needs to find peak fitness and sharpness before any real judgement can be made, and he's running out of time. The lack of goals is also a worry, as it was his strong suit at Leeds and in his first year at Liverpool, before the curse struck.

Andrei Voronin started his Liverpool career well, and has had a few excellent games, but has recently trailed off into oblivion. Again, it's hard to know what to make of him, and his lack of cachet amongst the fans makes him an easy target. A decent acquisition as a free transfer, he could just be going through the adaptation process; but as a free transfer he'll always be regarded with scepticism. It's hard to see past him being fourth-choice at best.

John Arne Riise's form has also disintegrated. Never the greatest player, he had a couple of very solid seasons at left-back under Rafa, and has weighed in with some important goals. Maybe he needs a new challenge?

In the same position, Fabio Aurelio has excellent technique, and put in his best display for the Reds at Manchester City. But long-term fitness concerns have hampered his progress. When he plays like he did at the Eastlands you can see someone who is easily good enough, *if* he can stay fit. Arbeloa is also very good in the role, and perhaps more likely to nail it down, given his good fitness record and extra pace. Meanwhile, 18-year-old Insua may make the breakthrough in the next year or two.

Jermaine Pennant is another 'nearly' player. He has pace, good control, can beat a man and deliver a really telling cross. But when not on form his game can fall apart (as it can with 'confidence' players), and his lack of any kind of goal threat is clearly a problem. His problem is being compared with someone like Ronaldo — the kind of player you can't easily get hold of.

Pennant was excellent in the second half of last season, and man-of-the-match in the Champions AC Milan. He started this season well, but his form dipped before injury struck. He remains a good option, but until he finds a consistent end product, nothing more.

Sebastian Leto, meanwhile, has yet to make any kind of impact, but has shown for the reserves that he has natural talent; at just 20, and adapting to life in England, that's maybe all we could hope for at this stage, from a player who was never bought as a potential world-beater in the first place.

Despite the current state of doom and gloom, I am convinced that the bones of a great team is there, and that a fair bit of it has been fleshed out, too. If the solution to who partners Torres, and how they perform, can be sorted, and Babel can progress either on the wing or in that very role, then that will be another step forward.

In the meantime, there may be nothing else to do, other than be patient.